A Lifetime of Fishing

David Dennis

Copyright © David Dennis, 2021

First Published in Ireland, in 2021, in co-operation with
Choice Publishing, Drogheda, County Louth, Republic of Ireland.
www.choicepublishing.ie

Paperback ISBN: 978-1-913275-44-0

eBook ISBN: 978-1-913275-45-7

All rights reserved. No part of this publication may be reproduced, stored in a retrieval system, transmitted in any form, or by any means, electronic, mechanical, photocopying, recording or otherwise, without the prior permission of the copyright holder.

A CIP catalogue record for this book is available from the National Library.

Cover Photo: The 2nd round of the World Lure Championships in Bosnia, where I had a total of 21 trout in a 45 minute round.
Photo courtesy of Ivan Isanovic.

This book is dedicated to my son and daughter Rod and Annette who are so happy that I didn't choose those names.

To Tommy and Abygail and Caroline,
Thank you for understanding.

CONTENTS

FOREWORD	vi
INTRODUCTION	ix
SEASONS BEGINNINGS	01
TROUT – BACK IN THE DAY	06
BIG BROWN TALE	10
SEA TROUT LURES	14
LURE PRESENTATION, TROUT.	17
THE FLOATING ROD (Walthamstow Reservoirs)	19
THE NEW RIVER	22
LOUGH CORRIB MAYFLY (The truth)	24
CARP???	27
WORLD LURE CHAMPIONSHIPS – LIVING THE DREAM.	30
QUALIFYING HEATS	34
NEW BREED OF ANGLER – TECHNO TECHNO TECHNO TECHNO.	39
PERCH The final frontier	43
MY FIRST 20LB+ PIKE - THE STRUGGLE IS REAL	53
BATHTUB PIKE	57
BIG PIKE, SMALL LAKES	58

YOU NEVER KNOW	62
INFLATABLE FUN	64
PIKE - Dead baiting	67
THE GETAWAY BOAT	71
PIKE... BOAT FISHING (Tournaments)	73
CAROLINE'S PIKE	76
PIKE COMPETITIONS (Bank)	79
EAST COAST	83
TOPE	85
BASS	92
MULLET	97
TRAWLER STORY	102

FOREWORD

For some people, fishing is a great pastime/hobby. The pleasure that comes from catching a fish with rod, line, and hook is immense for those in the know. For some lucky people, it is a lifestyle choice, where time and motivation allows them to pursue their dreams. I am one of the lucky ones and on my travels, I have met many dedicated anglers in the same boat so they kind of justify the sometimes guilty passion we all share. I say guilty passion as sometimes when we are meant to be doing other things, probably important everyday things like work, spending time with family members, social occasions, etc the draw of fishing is too strong for us (anglers) to resist. We can always justify our excuses later, but don't worry too much, as God is lodging all these days in our deposit account and they get added back on to your life when you need them the most. This guilty passion (fever) has been taken to the extreme many times, even by close friends of mine that really should know better, just ask their almost ex-wives.

As an all-round angler, I'll probably slip in and out of the different disciplines of angling. Rivers, lakes, canals, sea fishing, etc and all of the predatory species that I fish for. I'm not much interested in the non-predatory fish species, as they normally don't savage your lure, chew it up and spit it back at you. Fishing with lures is the most exciting way of catching these predatory fish. It's been said before that when you get the hit (bite) it's an instant natural adrenaline rush to the brain. Oh yeah' and even just thinking about it is exciting. Lure fishing, casting artificial baits, mimicking living creatures, fish, flies etc adds a totally different dimension to angling, other than just catching fish. It's like a secret code that needs thoughts and ideas to figure it out. Fishing your lures through the water columns, trying to induce a reaction and find a depth where the fish are holding up. On any day, this may take minutes or hours, but when you get that adrenaline hit, instantly you are almost in another dimension, an otherworldly experience that brings you to the edge of our very existence as hunter-gatherers, part of the natural world since the beginning of time. BOOM! Fish on. You and the fish at either end of the line, and for a few fleeting moments, the balance is there, who wins? Does it matter? YES. Hopefully, on the next cast as that's the buzz we're all looking for. Like everything else, moderation is the key but I think the fish know this more than we do, and they don't let us get overly addicted to our passion, It's nature's way. Keeping all the Macky bashers over at the local harbour while you and I are over on the rocks looking for one pollack or wrasse. Of course, we don't want a fish every cast as it would become so boring that there would be no fun in it. Like picking sweets from a chocolate box, the first few are pleasing but then the pleasure wears off quickly. Luckily for us anglers, the fish and nature mostly decide the outcome of our fishing trips. So much so that on a given day when the fish are "ON" the take, we return to the same spot the next day fully armoured up with all our very best tackle for the "catching" and the fish refuse to cooperate full stop, story of my life.

The most interesting fishing days are when the fish don't want to cooperate with us. Even if you were to offer them three wishes from your lucky leprechaun in exchange for a bite they continue to completely ignore everything you throw at them. They can be so stubborn, it almost feels like you have offended them in some way. This being snubbed can last for days or weeks sometimes. It's like when your wife snubs you for absolutely no apparent reason and you're left standing there scratching your head trying to figure out why? So it is with fishing my friends.

What can you do? Thankfully, I only have an occasional, shall we say, stubborn day, while others suffer many blank sessions one after the other. If you find yourself blanking on numerous days my advice to you is to find a new place to fish, or return to an old venue that has produced success in the past. This will restore your fishing mojo, it's like a spell being broken and you'll forget all about those annoying blank sessions. On the other hand, if you continue blanking, then maybe you need a different hobby.

INTRODUCTION

We're all in this together boys and girls.

To begin. Most of the content of this book is based around the Boyne Valley area on the east coast of Ireland and counties; Louth, Meath, Monaghan, Cavan and further afield.

The life of an all-round angler really is a fantastic voyage of discovery. I am not sure what it is that drives anglers like myself, I guess it's something like gold rush fever or something. It's the desire from within to catch such beautiful treasures that would otherwise remain unseen in almost every waterway, lough, or ocean. Inspiration from other anglers comes in exciting tales of great days fishing, or indeed the capture of a truly large specimen. It doesn't necessarily mean that the one who has caught the biggest fish is the greatest angler, they may well be a great angler but the fishing Gods ultimately decide our big fish quota. Or 'luck' in other words. Some say that it's better to be a lucky angler than a good angler, but if you are both lucky and good, then you are truly blessed.

SEASONS BEGINNINGS

I was introduced to angling by my Father, Tom. The first few trips were quite memorable, but for the wrong reasons, as I tripped and fell into the water on the first two out of three or four outings. I was about nine years old, and my soakings meant that he would have to cut his days fishing short. Not a good start. I was already thinking to myself *'is this fishing crack for me?'* Apart from the soakings, I would have gotten the cold shoulder from my older siblings for cutting their days fishing short too. So it was that I missed a few fishing trips, as I was much safer at home and dry.

My two older brothers, Pat and Paul, were a great inspiration to me as there was always great excitement when my father and brothers would arrive home with their catch. Brown trout from the river Boyne is one of the nicest table fish you can get. The delicate flavour and texture must be experienced to understand how good they actually taste. I apologise to all the catch and release purists, but there's more to fishing than just catching fish. April, May and June are the best of the months for dining on the brown trout, as later on in the year they take on a much stronger flavour that makes them less palatable. It's not possible to buy these fish, and it's sustainable fishing if only one or two are occasionally taken for the pot. They would also have sea trout or salmon depending on the time of year, also good for the table.

I had a lot to learn, and three better angling mentors I could not possibly wish for. Eventually, after a lot of pleading and promising to behave myself (i.e. not falling in), they began to bring me along more and more.

And within no time at all, I caught the bug for a lifetime's obsession with angling.

Tom Dennis at Clogherhead

If you put a rod into the right person's hand, it's almost like a magic wand is waved and they will be eternally grateful for it. I guess it's the same with other people if you give them a football. They'll all play with it for a while but there's always the one that stands out, with extra skills and control that comes naturally. My daughter, Abygail, was one of the stand out players. Skills and control just came naturally to her from a young age. In fact, the first word she ever said was 'ball' as a ball bounced by her pushchair one day. Arms stretched out, *"ball!"* she said. She went on to enjoy a great amateur level of playing soccer and is still playing today. She was the only girl amongst nine boys that represented Ireland in the Medtronic Diabetic World

Championships in 2012 which was held in Switzerland. Ireland finished a respectable 6th place out of twelve participating countries, from as far away as Canada would you believe. Non-inclusive to fishing, but worth mentioning whilst I'm at it, Abygail scored a cracker against Germany in the early rounds, and Germany went on to win the tournament overall. I must add that for the team Ireland selection, she was the only girl selected for the team. That was a fantastic trip of a lifetime and we all travelled over to Switzerland for it.

When I started fishing, it was always trout and salmon that were our target species. I was always more of a trout man while my brothers had a passion for salmon. Any legal method was used but I think fly fishing is ideally suited to trout fishing, and I was to become quite accomplished at this discipline of angling.

At the beginning of the season I would always start on the local reservoirs or the river Boyne, especially if it wasn't flooded as we get an abundance of rain here in Ireland. Even at a very young age, I could hardly wait for the season to start, St Patrick's day was normally our first outing. One year, I chanced to fish on the reservoir on the 1st February only to be put off by the caretaker, Paddy Wade. Around the end of June or start of July, the sea trout would arrive up the river Boyne in great numbers, and we experienced some phenomenal catches. Once I had mastered river fishing, there were almost unlimited numbers of trout to be caught. Being off school for three months every summer, myself and good friend, Derek, spent many summers practically living on the banks of the Boyne. The sea trout fishing was in the tidal reaches, so sometimes we would fish both the early morning tide (6am-11am) and again later in the day (6pm-11pm). This involved a lot of cycling. Getting home around midday for something to eat and maybe a nap, then back out for the evening session. By the end of those seasons, my fishing trousers would be noticeably looser fitting as a result of the cycling I guess.

One summer, when I was 14 or 15 years old, I was meant to start back at school, usually around the 1st of September. That season hadn't been as good as usual and as luck would have it, the Trout and Salmon started arriving in good numbers a bit later than usual in the season. With the season then closing on the 15th September, I would have missed the best of the fishing that year. I was totally shocked when my Mother, Eileen, or commonly referred to by her nickname 'Ginger' said to me that I could stay off school until the 16th. I didn't need to be asked twice, I can tell you that for sure. It was sort of normal at the time such was the connection our family had with the river. My father, having grown up on Ship Street in Drogheda right on the banks of the Boyne, Draft net fishing for salmon was their livelihood, until he took a job in a local factory. The draft net fishing was a basic set up used to catch Salmon for thousands of years and involved the use of a small rowing boat and pulling a net across the river into a loop, then hauling it in from the shoreline. Thankfully, but also regrettably, this method has been stopped since 2007, as has the taking of any salmon from rivers on the east coast of Ireland, due to the very low numbers of returning salmon every year. Anglers must also release any rod caught salmon in an effort to conserve the already diminished stocks, and I myself haven't seen any improvement in the stocks in the fourteen years since the ban was put in place. There are still some salmon to be caught on rod and line, but nothing like the numbers there were thirty years ago. The river Boyne salmon are generally bigger in size than the west of Ireland salmon. Boyne salmon average out around 7lb weight with 20lb plus specimens, still being caught to this day.

Fishing for sea trout was usually carried out with worms and maggots as bait. Eventually, I started experimenting with small spinners and really enjoyed catching on a different method. Spinning and fly fishing are very similar. There's a lot of trout flies that are actually lures of a type, especially sea trout and salmon flies. Even to this day, I still cannot understand why spinning is frowned upon by fly fishing snobs. It would be just too difficult for them to admit that they're just fishing lures in a different way.

Also anglers using Maggots, yes you read it correctly, *maggots*, as trout bait, would have been known to scoff at the audacity of the spinning angler. Where these notions ever came from is beyond comprehension, but this sort of contempt for the spin fisher is unbelievably still alive and well in modern Ireland.

TROUT - Back in the day

Back in the day, late 70's early 80's, cycling was my only form of transport. In my early teenage years, I was lucky enough to live within cycling distance of three local reservoirs, (all of them part of the same system). The river Boyne and its attached canal system and the river Nanny all within 10 kilometres of my home.

Usually, I would have a friend or two tagging along for the crack but also would go solo sometimes.

Money wasn't very plentiful at the time and most of my tackle was from hand me downs and a general hotchpotch of whatever I could get my hands on. A decent fly set up would have cost a considerable amount of money, so, unlikely a 14-year-old fella like me would have one. My eldest brother, Patrick, kindly knocked together a sort of basic fly set up with an ancient reel and an old silk fly line. With the silk fly line, you could add grease/vaseline etc to make it float for later in the season or then wash it all out for earlier in the season so it would sink. Casting weights hadn't been invented then not to my knowledge anyway not that it would have mattered. Back in the day fishing tackle wasn't as easily accessible or affordable as it is these days.

And so I began fly fishing. No lessons, as I was so keen to get started I couldn't wait for my father or older brothers to show me the basics so they explained as best they could what to do and off I cycled up to Killineer reservoir on a solo trip to teach myself fly fishing. It didn't take me long to learn how to cast the old silk line, which I did need to rub vaseline into to make it float.

When I was false casting (that's, laying a cast on the water, adding more line and casting again and repeat as required to achieve the desired distance needed) up came a trout just when I was lifting into the back cast and I don't know who was more shocked, me or the trout. Fish on, and it was a good one. It must have been 14oz, which was a decent size for a non stocked reservoir (I don't think stocking was a big thing in the 70's) I played the trout very carefully to the net but somehow the line parted and I lost it. Probably due to wind knots on my first ever fly session. Gutted describes that particular feeling quite aptly, and on checking the leader a number of wind knots were present. However, I felt duly rewarded having hooked a decent trout on my first attempt at fly fishing and was well and truly hooked. Consulting with the rest of the family they informed me that my leader was too light for the task so I upped it to 5lbs B/S mono. I was also allowed to pick a duplicate of the same fly from my brother's fly collection. Off I cycled the very next day with great enthusiasm.

I spent a few hours casting with nothing to show for my efforts and I was losing interest when suddenly a trout showed up to my left in the margins. Instinctively I covered the trout with my next cast and again I was surprised when the trout turned on my fly. After a good scrap, I had a trout on the bank which was the biggest trout that I had ever seen coming out of the reservoir. 2 and a half pounds, absolutely mind-blowing to catch such a trout, from this venue and on the fly too. The rest as they say is history and it was the beginning of being well and truly hooked on fly fishing.

Arriving home with my catch I met my brother, Pat, parking his Honda 50 motorbike. He too had been fishing on the River Dee that day and said he had a nice sea trout. When we laid the two trout side by side they were almost identical in proportion except for the colouration which set them apart. Well, we were both truly blessed by the fishing Gods on that day. What a memory to cherish. I can remember that day like it was yesterday even though it was over forty years at the time of writing it down.

Killineer Reservoir, an idyllic trout fishery

I spent a lot of my youth on Killineer reservoir and if any of you reading this ever get a chance to visit it I would highly recommend it, as a more beautiful fishery you will not find, more especially on a sunny afternoon in the months of May and June when nature is in full flow and everything is bursting into life. Idyllic... Nowadays it's heavily stocked with rainbows and browns, the wild trout are still present but not as numerous as they were back in the day. The local anglers always used to talk about a stocking of trout that came from Loch Leven in Scotland. I can't imagine it myself but who knows. There is a different strain of trout present in the reservoir, fact. They have a silvery appearance. The locals always refer to these trout as 'Loch Levens'. In my opinion, they are sea trout from the feeder stream that supplies the water to the reservoir when the water levels are high enough for them to pass. The feeder stream is directly connected to the River Boyne system that still gets a great run of sea trout to this day. They then end up in the reservoir on their return trip, either way it's always a bonus to catch one.

BIG BROWN TALE

Having lived abroad for fourteen years, I returned to live in Ireland in the year 2000; I was keen to visit all of my old fishing haunts. There was and thankfully still is some fantastic fishing here in Ireland. The fishing in England (where I spent most time away) is also very good and the waterways very well managed and maintained. In Ireland it's all pretty much left to mother nature to do as she pleases. I often hear it being said that the English go fishing in their slippers whereas in Ireland Full Chest waders and wet suit are needed most of the time and can be very challenging fitness wise if fishing from the shores of the multitude of lakes that are completely wild with rough banks, drains, dykes, barbed wire fences, bog holes etc. A boat always comes in handy when available.

So, in 2001, the foot and mouth crisis hit our shores and brought Ireland and the UK to a standstill pretty much. I won't go into the details here but six million cows and sheep were killed to stop the spread of disease and all access to farm lands prohibited until April 21st 2002. That meant no fishing, all through the winter there was no pike fishing and roll onto March 2002, still no start of the trout season, a very difficult time for us anglers. Then news that April 21st was the date when everything would return to normal was very welcomed. I picked up my elder brother, who is Salmon mad, and off we went up the river. I dropped him off at a Salmon stretch and I went to a different river section that was more trouty. Both of us had fished on this wonderful river Boyne all our lives, as our Father did and his Father before him. It would be fair to say that we knew the river well. However, the unusual land closures due to the disease gave us river banks like we had never seen before. There had always been livestock grazing the fertile lands along the river banks but this year no livestock or footfall of any kind. Nature was in full blossom with high grass and wildflowers all along the banks. I remember thinking how beautiful it was as it should be. Natural beauty.

Along one stretch of 2-300meters long I tied a dry sedge onto my 5lb b/s leader. It's always a good one to start with in this section. I made a few practice casts to get my arm in but no sign of any trout on the surface. I was expecting a few to show as I was the very first person to have walked the bank in months.

In the distance at the other end of the stretch a big fish turned on the surface and I thought that it was a salmon as the trout average 1 - 2 lbs. I went to investigate and sure enough the fish rose again about 40 meters upstream. I crept up behind in the long grass keeping as low a profile as possible, made a cast and up came a huge brownie to about half an inch under my fly and turned away. Heart stopping to say the least and also very disappointing too. Was that my only chance? Then a short distance upstream a big rise, could it be the same fish? I crept up behind it again and watched and waited for the fish to show. I saw the fish take a natural fly from the surface then rise to another natural and not take it, then take another natural off the surface. I made a cast, no reaction, another cast was rejected. Then the big rise a short distance upstream again, of course I crept up behind it again and covered it and no reaction from the trout. Strangely, there were no other fish showing on the whole of the stretch. I would have noticed, as it was flat calm. Maybe the big brown was totally dominating the whole stretch and I had never seen a trout behave in this manner before or since then.

After following the trout all the way to the top of the stretch I could go no further due to bank side vegetation, trees and scrub etc. I assumed the fish would keep moving upstream as it had been. I sat down thinking about it all, I had come so close, three casts and three times I was denied. Sounds a bit biblical. I had been totally absorbed for the past hour or so and failed the exam miserably. **Trout 1, Me 0.**

Then, about ten minutes later, the same big rise back at the start of the stretch. Big brown trout on the river Boyne are notoriously shy creatures and normally you'll only get one good cast at them for the season. This year with land access prohibited the trout was feeding confidently in its element.

So, again to the start of the stretch, and again and again my offerings refused. Even changing flies would not tempt this magnificent beast of a brownie. All the way to the top of the stretch with the same result.

Ding, Ding, Round 3. Sitting at the top of the stretch the fish showed at the start where I had first spotted it. Off I went, at this time almost giving up all hope but persevered. I had stopped creeping and was now standing upright and walking instead of crawling after the fish every time she rose, always moving upstream I would cover her. I tied on a favourite dry daddy long legs and to my surprise up she came and sucked it in.

Well, hell hath no fury like this beast, going completely mental on me. I could hardly believe I hooked and eventually landed it. Luckily I had a camera and got a decent old school snap. (remember no phone cameras back then). It weighed in at 5lb 14oz of pure wild Boyne brown trout. One quick photo was normal back in the day when we had a 24 actual film roll in the camera and a quick release, never to be seen again. A very special trout and memory from twenty years previous and I can recall it like it had happened today.

Twenty years of fishing the Boyne since then and just last year in 2020, I caught a 5lb 5oz Brownie. Great to see that the river is in good order still producing magnificent specimens.

Big Boyne Brownie, 5lb 14oz, April 2001

SEA TROUT LURES

It's hard to better the old standard lures like a no.1or no.2 mepps blue and silver or a Rapala countdown 3cm or 5cm or Rapala ultra light minnow. There are many many different manufacturers with similar or sometimes better lures but in general the old standards do the job quite well and are reasonably priced so loosing an odd one here and there is ok. Some of the better made hard plastic lures from Japan are almost too expensive, 14 euro maybe for one. If you were to lose a couple every time you went fishing it would add up to a considerable amount by the end of the season. Japan is now the world leader in producing the best hard plastics available. The engineering in every different lure is truly amazing. When you spend that 14 euro it's a quality product. One such lure that's always the first out of my box is the Ryuki spearhead 50mm yaname pattern. Trout and sea trout can barely resist the action of this lure. Similar in looks and size to most hard plastics its very different to a rapala. The rapala can work well on a straight retrieve with a great wobbling action that the trout love. The Spearhead on a straight retrieve will almost have no wobble. It must be activated by short sharp pulls to wobble it and aggressive jerks on the rod to get it to dance like an injured bait fish. This particular lure can also be fished casting downstream and working it back upstream. Another string to your bow.

Lures will catch better when the river is slightly higher than normal levels. When the water levels are normal or low the trout and sea trout in particular are very finicky and it's usually only the first cast you get in a chosen swim that will get a reaction. If you get a hookup then well done but if a trout or three appear darting like bullets around your lure do not make another cast. Easy to say but not easy not to cast again. I've been doing it so long now and still at times I go for the next cast and realise I've messed up the swim. If you have had a follow just walk away and return sometime later an hour or more. If you think about it, if you've covered the swim with half a dozen casts and not had an offer, knock or follow then its most likely not going to happen. You'll need to move. Even if it's only 5 or 10 meters. Don't stand in the same spot you caught a fish in last week for half of the day. Move. The sea trout in the tidal stretches can only be caught when the tide is out. When the tide is in I guess they go travelling up and back downriver to the sea. They tend to hold in an area when the tide is out. It's always best to get first crack at a swim just as the tide has come off it, before anyone else goes in and messes it up. You'll soon learn where exactly to cast your lure to get a reaction and the first cast will be the most important cast in every new swim. The same rules apply for big brown trout in the normal, non tidal stretches. You might see them once or twice in a season and if they don't get hooked properly then you'll probably never see them again. They can be super shy creatures. Of course when there's more water in the river they drop their guard a little so maybe a better chance for a hookup then. The same lures can be used in the sea but I've found it difficult to actually land the sea trout in the sea as they go absolutely mental in the shallow water jumping and thrashing about usually ripping the hooks out of their mouths. It is my opinion that their mouths are softer in the seawater. Lighter monofilament and a lighter rod would help but they don't lend themselves well to the harsh sea environment, as I found out fishing from the beach one day when I hooked the biggest sea trout I've ever seen in the flesh (approximately 7 lbs) and of course I got broken off with my 4lb breaking strain mono. Don't go there. I recommend an 8lb minimum mono leader and light braid for its better casting characteristics.

Sea trout in the sea prefer rocky outcrops where they meet sandy beaches. The same as bass and if there's any kind of freshwater stream feeding into the sea then it's even better for sea trout as they congregate around the freshwater inlets. It's always worth watching your lure as it nears the rod tip for follows and the trout are moving so fast that you won't even see them if you're not 100% focused. If you've noticed one or two around and not had any knocks then try speeding up the retrieve even sweeping the rod back, while reeling for some extra speed, can sometimes induce a bite. The faster the better, and have the drag set very very loosely.

50cm fresh run river Boyne sea trout

LURE PRESENTATION, TROUT.

Early in the season from March 1st, the river trout will be hungry after a long cold winter. They will be searching the bottom layers of the river for nymphs, louse and minnows etc. Even the minnows and sticklebacks are deeper and you probably won't actually see any until the water temperatures rise in May/June when they can be clearly seen in the margins. The river Boyne is a big river and depths averaging 5-6ft in the trouty areas (there are also very deep stretches that are not suitable for targeting trout but do hold some huge specimens) Lures must be presented in the bottom layers of the river to be fishing effectively. Heavier spinners 10 gram, and deeper diving crank baits like rapala countdowns are great for searching the deeper stretches. Small coloured tungsten jig heads with shads, nymphs, grubs and paddle tail lures etc will work well when you really need to scrape the bottom for a bite. This style of fishing for trout is relatively new to us in Ireland and an exciting new method if you've never tried it. Ultra light rods and reels give great sport from even the smallest of trout. The Hi-viz line is a great advantage as it will tell where your lure is, and observing the line for gentle bites. A light clear fluorocarbon leader will be needed to attach your lure so as not to spook the trout. This has the obvious advantage of being less visible but also very useful when fishing small nymphs, grubs etc. If you have a two meter long fluorocarbon leader and a one gram jig head with nymph, the hi-viz gives good indication of the depth your jig head is fishing. Holding the rod high and adjusting with the flow makes it a lot easier to present the nymph correctly. Any sign of the hi-viz twitching, stopping or moving at all could be a bite and a short lift of the rod will confirm if it is a bite. Jig head weights depend on the flow and sometimes half a gram or less is needed and up to maybe 3 grams for the heaviest flow. As the season progresses and the water levels drop and slow down it's important to scale everything down to finer leaders and smaller lures, spinners, with smaller hooks.

An average sized fresh run sea trout from the river Boyne.

THE FLOATING ROD
(Walthamstow Reservoirs)

Back in the day B.C. before children and before everything became P.C. I was courting my wife Caroline. We were both living in London and I really cherished my weekly visits to Walthamstow reservoirs, ahem, my weekly date nights with Caroline. It's a fantastic area of modern engineering (from 1853 onwards I believe) and a great wildlife sanctuary right in the middle of the Metropolis of London. I'm sure many of you reading this would have brought your lifelong partners fishing in the early days when you started dating. It would be interesting to see what percentage of couples, that had those early fishing trips, are still together now and for how long. Are the early fishing trips real building blocks for long lasting relationships? Something built into us naturally, the old hunter gatherer theory ingrained into our psyche. We all know that Zen like feeling that comes occasionally when surrounded by nature and time stands still. Magic moments. I once heard somewhere (can't recall where) that all the time we spend fishing is added back on at the end of our lives. So, don't feel guilty as fishing is the best excuse for days and even weekends away from home. *'Sure, I could be doing a lot worse'* is the excuse I give to Caroline if she has a little bit of a gripe about me heading off on yet another fishing trip.

On one of our trips to Walthamstow Reservoirs in London (Reservoir No.4). I had a ramshackle collection of tackle most of which I acquired from an old house I had been renovating in Chislehurst. Also some odds and ends acquired from boot sales etc. Decent fishing tackle was a lot more expensive back then unlike today's modern throwaway world.

A 13ft glass float rod with a rubbish reel loaded with 10lb or so mono was set ledgering with sweetcorn as bait. I had a lighter leader on with a running ledger. Also I had a spinning set up of sorts and a fly set up. I was showing Caroline a few tricks with the fly rod as she was enjoying the fly fishing as it was more interactive though no fish came to the fly, or anything else that day. Not the dreaded blank, my future lifelong relationship hanging delicately in the balance right there. I guess a trout must have risen up to our left as we were about 30 meters away from the ledgering rod. When we returned we were very surprised. The ledgering rod had vanished. I scanned the water and about 40-50 meters out in the ripple I could barely make out what must be the floating rod slowly moving upwind. Amazed it actually floated. I quickly tied on a no.3 mepps onto the spinning gear and first cast snagged the line on the floating rod and retrieved it. It still had the 3.5lb rainbow attached to about 100 meter of mono and managed to land it. It was great excitement altogether, from being fishless, losing a rod and reel and catching a lovely rainbow trout and rescuing the rod and reel. It's the simple things in life that really matter the most, for me, a truly wondrous series of events.

For me, Walthamstow reservoirs were an oasis in the middle of the everyday madness, and believe me, madness was a thing I was doing a lot of during that time living in London as a young singleton. I did enjoy the madness but Walthamstow Ressies were the sanity I needed to keep me grounded. No.4 and No.5 reservoirs would produce some monster rainbows during the month of October for about two weeks the resident rainbows would go on the rampage. I witnessed one of 12lb being caught. I hooked a couple of these beasts on the fly gear and never experienced anything like it before or since then. They went absolutely ballistic and smashed my 5lb B/S leaders before I knew what was going on. Of course I returned the following weekend properly armoured up for these beasts, but the short window of the showing of these big fish had passed. That's fishing.

THE NEW RIVER

Lady luck was to shine on me again when Caroline and I bought our first home in London N'22. With our first baby on the way we were both in separate rental accommodation so given the circumstances it was time to grow up. Mortgage time. No more dead rental money paying someone else's mortgage. After many viewings in north London our offer on a ground floor two bed maisonette was accepted and our new life together began.

Not being familiar with the local area we went for a walkabout. It looked like a decent enough residential area with mostly Victorian style houses converted to maisonettes. Not far from our house we came across a small bridge, and guess what else? A nicely flowing river, I could not believe my luck when I could see small shoals of roach from the bridge, and our back garden was only a stone's throw from it right in the London suburbs. Access however was strictly prohibited but I'm an angling addict so I'm sorry but those rules don't apply. The water in the New River was always crystal clear and almost aquarium-like. This meant that the fish in it were not easy to catch as I was to learn that usually, if you can see fish then they can see you and for whatever the reason they are very difficult to tempt on any bait if you are looking directly at them. Small roach, perch and jack pike were the normal catch with an odd bigger specimen showing up but again almost impossible to catch but more than enough to keep me occupied in the sometimes stifling formality of city living. As access was prohibited I had about a half a kilometre between the bridges mostly all to myself and occasionally another angler. My own little fishing oasis in the heart of suburbia. An idyllic getaway for the angling addict. One day I ventured across the north circular road upstream. The river was very different in that section with concrete embankments and industrial pumping machinery etc. Not many fish either except the two biggest perch I've ever seen in my life. What a sight in the crystal clear water. They had to be 4lb'rs. Going casually about their business until they became aware of me and they were gone. That was in 1997, Recently 2021 a 5lb 6oz urban perch was recorded caught in London and rumour has it that it was from the New River, I for one believe it. I'd love to get a few days on it again, with permission granted of course.

Back garden fishing, the New River

LOUGH CORRIB MAYFLY
(The truth)

Good fortune was to shine on me again when I started my current employment as my workmate owned a cabin on the shores of Lough Corrib. It's not a very exciting job but we get to travel all over the country fitting storage cabinets in hospitals and ambulance depots. Sometimes in the Galway area and an odd overnight or two night stay is needed to complete the job in hand. With the longer evenings of late May and early June when the mayfly get going the cabin is the ideal choice of accommodation and much less expensive than hotels in the city centre.

Over the years I've had a good few mayfly sessions and can honestly say that a lot of luck is needed to hit it right. Usually, we would only get an evening and a half day fishing the next day so not really enough time. I guess a full week at least would be needed to actually experience the mayfly fishing properly as it peaks and troughs depending on the weather each day.

So many times we tried and the weather was against us. But, there was always O'Malley's pub in Cornamona as a backup venue and some great fishing was done in there over the years!! The locals are well used to visiting anglers and their stories about great trout being caught and everyone gets their podium moment. The locals have heard it all before and can stop a fella in mid story with a simple question. Did You See It?

Incidentally, in O'Malley's pub, they have a stuffed Pike of absolutely monstrous proportions. And yes, I did see it. I think it weighs an unbelievable 48lbs.

While I'm on the subject of Corrib pike I have a stuffed pike mounted on my kitchen wall that was gifted to me by the captors' son (my work buddy) for safekeeping. Dom's father, Phil Gradwell, amazingly caught the 26lb pike whilst Mayfly fishing for trout some years earlier. An awesome catch that took great skill to land on light trout tackle.

Even with the weather usually against us we would normally manage to catch one or two trout.

One day though, all the jigsaw pieces fell into place. The previous evening we put in a few hours with only a small keeper to Dom's rod, and of course I was frequently reminded all evening 1-0 and so on. The next day the sun was up, with a light breeze blowing warmly across the Lough and, from the first drift the trout were on. Finally, this was The Mayfly on Lough Corrib that I had heard so much about for all of my life. I have to say it was some of the most enjoyable exciting fishing I've ever experienced.

Dapping is the traditional method practised by local fishermen since the beginning of time. It involves gathering mayflies from the shoreline as they hatch and float ashore with the wind, and then clamber out onto the rocks and long grassy margins to dry out. They complete their magical transformation from underwater nymph into the adult mayfly. Collecting these mayfly is an enjoyable pastime in its own right as you become part of the whole cycle of life. Some very elaborately constructed homemade boxes are used to store the mayfly and keep them in pristine condition for fishing up to a day later. It is normal to put two of them on a size 12 hook so as to give the trout a bit more of a mouthful and also visually a slightly bigger profile therefore more visible.

Drifting downwind, the trout are moving upwind towards the boat. Keeping the mayfly dapping the surface, and a gentle lift of the rod to let the wind carry it to full reach, dap it again and repeat. The exciting bit is when you see a trout rise maybe 30 meters downwind and you adjust your cast as best you can. The expectation being fulfilled when the trout sucks in your fly, wait a second and lift. Fish on. Phenomenal. This happened more than fourteen times during that four hour session, landing fourteen trout up to 2lbs in weight. My friend, Dom, wasn't so lucky, only landing one undersized trout for the session. I reminded him of the one he caught on the previous day which he repeatedly mentioned in the pub the night before. I even offered him some of my catch before releasing them but he quietly and politely refused stating that he'd prefer to catch his own trout for the table. I kept a couple of pan sized ones for myself and all else released with due care. They are one of the finest table fish at this time of year as they are in their prime. I've tried eating them at the back end of the season and the flavour is too strong and best to release them for next year. Out of ten or so short sessions, only once did it all come right, but, when it did happen it was a moment in time to treasure forever.

CARP???

One day, pulling lures (fly fishing) on number 5 Reservoir Walthamstow, all was quiet. Not a single knock. Then my 7 weight fly rod buckled over and the line screamed off the reel. One long uninterrupted run in a straight line. I guessed it wasn't a trout as did the angler next to me who said you'll never land that thing on a 5lb leader. Now, I've landed some fierce fighting fish on very light tackle and was ready for the challenge. There were some very large carp in no.5 and I knew that somehow I had one on the fly rod. On the first run it looked like the carp was going to spool me. That's 30 meters of fly line and 100 meters of backing as spooled in the shop, when I bought it from Don's of Edmonton. I remember asking him when he was spooling the reel, do I need a hundred meters of backing? And his answer, Well, you never know do you. Feathering the spool as much as I dared I thought I'd had it, watching the final few coils on the bottom of the spool with only inches left, and the carp stopped. Quickly I inched some line back onto the reel and strangely managed to get the carp to within 30 meters of the bank and off she went again on a slightly shorter run 80 meters maybe.

To cut a long story short, every subsequent run would get shorter and shorter. After a while a small gathering of people had arrived to witness this monster of the deep, some stayed for half an hour maybe before moving on. My angler friend (The challenger) was still there. I could get the carp to the edge of an underwater shelf and the fish would lodge itself there not moving at all for long periods and about 4 times I lobbed a big stone as near as I could to where the fish was. Amazingly every time I did this the fish would take off on another run.

One hour and thirty five minutes later I had my first mirror carp in the net. What a battle. The carp lads had heard the commotion and had come over from no.3 ressie and they estimated it around 25lb in weight. My angler friend (the challenger) was gone. The carp had been hooked in the tail (fish fight longer and harder when foul hooked). What a memory from all those years ago, it's like it was yesterday.

Carp on the fly

Don's of Edmonton was a real gem of a tackle shop. When I was buying my first properly set-up, balanced fly outfit he brought me onto a green area at the back of the shop, with no sign of water anywhere, surrounded by apartments (flats we used to call them).

I tried out different rod lines, casting weights etc until I found one I liked. Sadly it closed sometime in the early 2000's. It was Don himself that recommended the professor spoon to me as a great pike taker and again he was 100% correct and to this day some 30 years on, the professor spoon is still one of my go to lures. Take note please. As I said a great shop and great service and it will be sadly missed. The two old boys that ran the shop were straight out of a Mr.Crabtree book or J.R.Hartley's Fly fishing. Absolute gentlemen.

WORLD LURE CHAMPIONSHIPS.
LIVING THE DREAM.

My favourite type of fishing is with lures. Spinning or fly, same thing, same rules apply. I know the fly schnobs won't agree and are probably ripping pages out of my book and setting them alight. But, deep down inside their psyche they know it's true. Then, the fly angler that posts his photo of 150lb blue shark caught on the fly. I'm not even wasting any more ink on that subject. Apart from them probably killing the shark playing around with it on much too light tackle.

Lures are without a doubt the most enjoyable and fun form of angling. I've mostly given up on fly fishing due to problems with my shoulders and elbows probably caused in part by fly casting but also working with power tools all of my life. So, thank God for the light lure set ups that are so ultra light they can be used all day long with absolutely no fatigue or muscle pain.

The days when you hit on the right lure are magical. The regular tried and tested lures don't always work and the fun bit is trying to discover the lure of the day. Chopping and changing retrieves, depths, sizes, colours, trying to get a bite. Subconsciously, all that you already know is running in the background but nothing is coming to your lures. I know guys that can adapt so quickly to any given situation, I think it's called Watercraft, it seems more like witchcraft to me at times. They know that tiny changes in weather conditions can bring the fish on, and they will be ready as soon as the wind picks up. Meanwhile the rest of us are wondering what colour lure we will try next.

Team Ireland at the World Lure Championships 2018
Back row left to right: Andrew Powell, Simon Gibson,
David Dennis, Jacek Gorney.
Front row: Colin Rutherford, Tomek Kurman, Steven Powell.

In my opinion Lure colour is not as important as it's made out to be. Sometimes yes, but it's more about size, shape, depth and speed can be a very important factor with lures. For instance static fishing a creature bait for perch or in contrast milking the cow with a big black minky for stockie rainbows, both are very effective on the right day, it's all about knowing when to change. Sometimes with slight weather changes, air pressure etc completely turn the fish, on or off the bite. The most important thing to remember when lure fishing is that it's all about having fun, and it can be very frustrating and annoying at times and when that happens you've lost the game completely. I've seen grown men going to pieces on their brand new boat, new fish finders, new engine, all the latest new lures that money can buy, but they can't buy a bite for love or money. Remember guys, this is where the patience bit comes into the fishing. The patience that everyone talks about. *'Oooooh he must be a very patient man, he's always out fishing.'* Patience is needed when you get into one tangle after another and then snagged on the bottom and loose your favourite lure and miss that big fish of a lifetime and the engine won't start, or, stop and then your mate gets a new PB and your new boots leaking the first time you wear them. Now, patience must always prevail, if you are to succeed in competitions. Never take your eyes off your opponent, every conceivable annoyance should wash straight over your head. Bruce Lee had similar encouragement from grand master Wing Chung in the 70's movie classic, Enter the Dragon (I watched this movie in the cinema at the time and it had a remarkable impact on me and all of my friends.) In our chosen field of fishing with lures there are some truly great masters of the sport. I've competed with and against some of the worlds greatest lure anglers and time and again their skills show them at a higher level of understanding, easily manipulating every factor possible on the competition days to finish in a podium position. The Russian lure master Alexi Shannin won both the bank and boat World Championship titles. I still dream about winning the world championships, but age is against me as I think I was possibly the oldest competitor entered into the event on the last few trips. But, hey. I've made the Irish team eight times so far, eight World Championships and have no intention of hanging my rod up yet. I even had a 1st place position one year in one round out of eight rounds finishing ahead of some true masters like Peter Hornack from Slovakia. He went on to win the World championships the next year. I love it.

Team Ireland at the 2019 World Lure Championships in South Africa. Left to right: Tomek Kurman, Simon Gibson, Steven Powell, David Dennis, Jacek Gorney.

These men (they are referred to as athletes at the world championships) are at the very top of their game and if it were a different sport such as boxing, tennis or golf then they would be household names.

Our sport unfortunately will never make the Olympic Games in its present form because of the fact that we are sticking hooks into live creatures and not acceptable under current Olympic legislation. We may see some angling in the Olympic Games in the form of casting techniques Fly or beach or performance casting etc. Not for me though.

QUALIFYING HEATS

For anyone thinking of entering the qualifying heats for the world championships please contact me via social media and I will do my very best to get you started. At first glance the rules for entry level are overwhelming. So many seemingly ridiculous rules that would put most people off entering. However, these are the same rules of the world championships (set by the International Olympic Committee) and it's important to familiarise yourself with the rules from the beginning. It does take some time to adjust to the rules but they are paramount in order to ensure standards are maintained. Also, the scoring and penalty points system is designed to eliminate the lucky one off angler that happens by chance to catch a few big fish to give them a 1st or place position. So, luck doesn't count much at this level. The same rules apply at the qualifying heats so nothing is left to chance or luck. Only skill will do it.

Representing Ireland on the world stage has been the absolute highlight of my fishing adventures, it was a great honour to represent my country, and as a team member the experience has really improved my lure angling abilities and has taken me to another level of angling. Also the experience has brought me to many different countries to compete internationally, that were not on my to do lists, such as qualifying for Bulgaria in 2014, Estonia in 2015, Slovakia in 2016, Bosnia in 2018 and most recently South Africa/ France/England.

I really wasn't prepared the first time I qualified for the WBC's in 2014 In Bulgaria. But, like everything in life you have to start at the bottom and persevere.

These world championship trips would normally take six days with two days of competition (possibly being extended to three days in the future) It might sound like ahh that'll be a nice trip away with the lads, bit of sightseeing etc but that hasn't happened yet. It is non-stop intense fishing right from when the team meets at the airport until the return trip after the main event. Every single moment is spent preparing, practising, discussing tackle and tactics. Fishing from dawn until dusk outside of the competition zones, official meetings and opening and closing ceremonies, its full on, sometimes struggling to find time to eat. We would normally hire a holiday cabin and everything gets shared out equally including all the best fishing tips and tricks and knowledge. You must be more than passionate about your fishing at this level. For me, it's living the dream.

It being my first time competing at world level, I was dropped off at my competition zone. Being away from the rest of the team I suddenly realised the mammoth task in front of me. What was I doing here? Competing in the world championships? It's no surprise that I almost had an accident in the trousers department. The pre-match nerves did unsettle me, but what a buzz. Just me against sixteen of the world's best lure anglers. 8 x 45 minute rounds over two days of the most intense fishing. It didn't go very well for me, but in the last round I completely changed tactics and caught five trout. I actually won that round sharing the top spot with another angler, so, a joint 1st place. But hey, a win is a win. My proudest fishing moment that I will probably not improve on, but I will keep trying. That first year for team Ireland we finished 15th of 17 countries.

XII Carnivorous Artificial Bait Shore Angling World Championships 2014
Asenovgrad - Bulgaria

Date: 17-05-2014
Leg nr.: 1
Sector: A
Round: Turno 4

Back Number	Competitor Angling	Team (Nation)		Valid Catches	Penalties (session)	Note
8	DENNIS David	Ireland		5	1.5	
15	LIPINSKI Andrzej	Poland		5	1.5	
1	CALU Morgan	France		4	3.5	
4	VOROBIEV Alexander	Russia		4	3.5	
2	LASTRIC Petar	Bosnia Herzegovina		3	6.5	
14	FERNANDES Fernando	Portugal		3	6.5	
7	KUK Željko	Croatia		3	6.5	
17	MUIN Giacomo	Italy		3	6.5	
5	BOYADZHIEV Lyubomir	Bulgaria		2	10.5	
6	POTYLYTSKYI Denis	Ukraine		2	10.5	
16	RIZEA Cristian	Romania		2	10.5	
13	CIRCENIS Ugis	Latvia		2	10.5	
9	GYVANYAM Bat	Mongolia		1	14.5	
10	TIBULCO Taras	Moldova		1	14.5	
12	KOLDYCHEVSKY Nikolay	Belarus		1	14.5	
3	HORNAK Peter	Slovakia		1	14.5	
11	CEPELÁK Tomáš	Czech Republic		0	17	C

Time: 14:48:01

President of Jury

16th Carnivorous Artificial Bait Shore Angling World Championship 2018
Želijeznica River - East Sarajevo

Sector B

Date: 26-05-2018
Organization: Bosnia Herzegovina
Period nr. 2
Leg nr. 1

Ranking	Angler	Nation	Fish (Nr.)	First start number	Note
1	HERRMANN Arno	Italy	22	9	
2	DENNIS David	Ireland	21	10	
3	MALUTAN Paul-Cristian	Romania	15	8	
4	BORAS Mijo	Croatia	14	14	
5	SEGUIN Jeremy	France	11	11	
6	HORNÁK Peter	Slovakia	10	15	
7,5	POHOSTINSKYI Kyrylo	Ukraine	9	5	
7,5	TIBULCO Taras	Moldova	9	18	
10	FOLTÝN Martin	Czech Republic	8	6	
10	IVASHKOV Alexey	Russia	8	17	
10	KOSTADINOV Todor	Bulgaria	8	4	
12,5	MAZUR Sebastian	Poland	7	2	
12,5	LUKIC Nikola	Serbia	7	13	
14	KRAJIŠNIK Igor	Bosnia Herzegovina	6	3	
15	SILVA António	Portugal	5	1	
16	PLANK Zoltán	Hungary	3	7	
17,5	JAKIMOVSKI Davor	Macedonia	2	12	
17,5	LEDOVSKYKH Valentiyn	Germany	2	16	
19	BERGMANIS Uno	Latvia	1	19	

Time: 13:10:53
President of Jury

Since then we have improved greatly and have finished mid table a few times now. We can achieve a podium position. We have the fishing part pretty much sorted and there's one major obstacle that we need to overcome to achieve our goal. Hopefully at the next event.

I mentioned the 8 X 45 minute rounds earlier. The numbers of trout needed for the early rounds can be insane. In the 2nd round at the event in Bosnia I had 21 trout in the 45 minutes time limit for a 2nd place. How close. A lucky Italian had 22 trout for a 1st position. I believe in the first round someone had 45 trout in 45 minutes. As I said, insane. As the rounds progress the numbers of fish being caught are fewer and fewer and by the last round it's difficult to get even one fish on the scoreboard. That year all our team members caught in every round and it's encouraging to see a great improvement for all our team combined efforts.

NEW BREED OF ANGLER.
TECHNO TECHNO TECHNO TECHNO.

With all of the new technology available today a new breed of angler has materialised. Without sounding like a proper old dinosaur I'm finding it hard to keep up with advances in technology. I'm not that worried about it as long as I'm still catching big fish. It's not all about fish finders and I pilots thank God. When I was a steward on the boat for Team England on Rutland Water, they brought the technology to the extreme for that event having no less than seven, yes, seven fish finders working at the same time. I was amazed looking at the screens while they were catching damn all. Technology? They also had radio headsets with bank runners keeping them updated on the whereabouts and catch rates of all other competitors. I think the results unfortunately show that the technology kind of got in the way of fishing. They finished 15th of 16 competing nations. At least they weren't last.

The most modern of fish finders now available look to be truly amazing with real time imaging, side imaging etc. I haven't used any of them so can't comment. Every few months there's new technology added and the prices of these units can only be justified by professional anglers. A university degree is also needed to operate and understand how they work. My current unit is a dragonfly pro 5 and is like a toy compared to more modern units. I have it about six years and it took me a while to understand what I was actually seeing on the screen but I use it to good effect now and wouldn't be without it... I'm probably slow to change but I reckon this surge in fishing technology probably coincided with the Celtic Tiger period up until 2007. Everyone was rich but didn't go fishing very often as they were too busy making money. Everything was just *'amazeballs'* as they said at the time and anyone could borrow unlimited amounts of money on loan from the banks. I'm getting off point here but honestly that was absolutely true at the time of the Celtic Tiger boom. Then the crash came in 2007. I didn't buy into the boom stuff as I had a mortgage and two children so tried to keep things real, right or wrong. There's two ways of looking at it, enjoy the excesses of endless loans and worry about it later, or, continue on the slow and steady stressless only buy what you can earn. I chose the latter but myself and Caroline were being offered huge amounts of ready cash at that time from the banks without even asking. As I'm sure everyone else in the country was. We ignored all of their offerings.

Social media and Google are fantastic tools for availing of fishing information and there are many experts sitting at their laptops right now. But, the old saying still holds true. You won't catch them sitting at home. Some people share information freely, while others have become very good at "Phishing" on social media. I guess it's the fisher in us that gets us scrutinising the background in the big fish photo, or the boat or maybe the lures etc.

When I caught my then PB pike of 29lb which was a significant capture at the time, I was amazed when a close friend told me that the 29lber I caught in March was the same fish I had caught at 25lb 9oz around the Christmas period. Now, I knew that it was the same fish as I would have compared photos to match individual markings so as to determine how many different big pike were in a particular venue. I was intrigued as to how he knew this, Mind Reading perhaps? He told me a mate of his told him. Now of course I hadn't told anyone so wondered how this was possible, and of course I had shared the photos on social media. Now his mate, whom I've only met once years ago, apparently was logging all of these big fish captures reported on social media and was able to tell that it was indeed the same fish. (You know who you are, and I have to say I found it a bit creepy at the time but it's now become kind of half normal behaviour on social media.) He forgot to mention though that I had caught her the previous February at 26lb 12oz or maybe he missed that one, slacking off there pal!

These repeat captures give us great insight into the life cycles of pike and add an extra interest to our pastime. It's a great bonus to recapture a big fish from maybe a year before and see that it's thriving (Showing that the particular venue is thriving) and growing in size despite being caught and released a few times. Cue the photo shoot with the pike unwittingly getting involved and gaining some form of celebrity status and much conversation in the piking community. That 29lber even made the front page of The Irish Anglers Digest (an actual printed magazine popular back then) I must bring a copy of it and get her to sign it if I bump into her again.

On another occasion a close friend had sent me a pm photo of his PB of 32lb plus. A great fish indeed and I duly congratulated him. A fish of a lifetime. He had also shared it on social media and within an hour he messaged me with the news that a well known piking celebrity of sorts was in contact with him (phishing I think it's called) and informed him that, That's David Dennis's 32lber and sure enough when I compared the photos it was the same fish.

And I thought I was obsessed, but no. Not compared to this level. It brings me some degree of happiness knowing that others are inflicted to a much greater degree of obsession than me. You know who you are readers…..Oh, and keep up the good work.

All of this is just a sign of the times when knowledge acquired over a lifetime of dedication (in all aspects of life) has taken a back seat to the mighty internet, Google etc are the new masters of the masses. Just go back fifty, no twenty odd years when my son

Tommy was born 1997. The general Joe public was only beginning to use the WWW dot and mobile phones were for making phone calls with text messaging being the latest technology available. So many advances since then.

PERCH - The final frontier

The last of the predatory species to attract my attention. Being successful at any of the angling disciplines requires a lot of commitment and dedication. Things to consider, firstly, time management. If you are a working man/woman with a young family fishing time will be limited to a few snatched hours here and there so, you must always be ready to take advantage of whatever time is available. This means having sufficient tackle in the car with rods already set up for any opportunity that arises. Also keeping a close eye on weather reports, water levels etc. Sometimes in summertime getting an hour in before work or a couple of hours after work. These are also usually the best times to be fishing. Luckily for the Perch I've left them well alone for most of my life but at present the humble Perch is my main target species from October to March and also through the summer months when they are at their most active. I started fishing for perch out of necessity as they are one of the predatory species that counted in the WBC's (world boat championships) also in the qualifying heats which are usually held in the summer months and pike can get very moody and difficult to catch during the summer so perch can add greatly to the scoreboard with some of the qualifying heats being won on just perch catches. And again, another chapter opened in my fishing life. I needed Perch.

They are truly the most beautiful of all of the freshwater fish, and a fully finned big one with full stripes and vivid red fins looks completely out of place compared to all other freshwater fish. Ok, Brown trout are equally beautiful but Perch are my new passion.

When I was about twelve years old and being raised on trout fishing on the local river, my Dad had left me along the bank and had moved upstream to try a different swim. It was standard practice back then to chuck out a ledgered worm and leave it sitting to wait for a bite. The fishing hole I was fishing is a well known salmon pool known locally as The Curley hole, and I got very excited when a bite registered on my rod. I undid the bail arm on the reel as per instructions and the line spooled off the reel. Of course I imagined a big salmon had taken my worm, it was a big lobworm possibly 7 inches long. Even at that tender age I was thinking big bait = big fish. I clipped over the bail arm tightened up and struck. Not the salmon I was expecting but I was totally amazed at the fish I now had in my hand. The worm was longer than it but I'd never seen anything like it. Like some alien fish or maybe from an aquarium. I unhooked it and excitedly ran up to my Dad to show him, unimpressed he said, *"have you never seen one of them before? It's a perch."*

In Ireland Perch don't grow as big as other European countries. A big Perch in Ireland would be a 2lb'er with 2lb 6oz being classed as specimen weight. The current Irish record is 5lb 9oz from the river Erne system. My personal best perch presently stands at 2lb 7oz and only 39 centimetres in length, so, of specimen size. Also a 2lb 6oz at 41cms and strangely a 43cms that only weighed in at 2lb 3oz. So far I've had only 3 perch at 43 centimetres in length with the heaviest going 2lb 6oz. Perches of this size are hard to come by so if you do, best to try and keep the location to yourself as I've foolishly shared one location and the word has spread far and wide. So much so that I've met Perch anglers on that venue that have travelled a great distance for a chance to catch one of that size.

As a result of the extra fishing pressure it has become very difficult to catch any size of perch in it. Perch are like that, once pressured they seem to vanish. However I have another couple of venues that also have good sized perch and I will definitely not share with anyone. That's my bass angler psyche kicking in there. Lately there have been a few 3lb plus perch (47 centimetres approximately) showing up on social media which is good news and a great inspiration for me to continue my Big perch search. (I have an active Facebook page titled Big perch search).

My PB perch at 45cms.

Lure fishing for perch is my preferred method and can be great fun when you cross over a shoal of decent sized ones willing to chomp on pretty much anything you throw at them, but then they can switch off like a light switch. Changing lures/colours/sizes methods will usually get a few more bites. A good basic set up to cover all the methods would be a 7ft light lure jigging rod with a casting weight up to 12 grams paired with a 2000 sized spinning reel, loaded with a hi/viz braid 0.1 diameter or roughly 10lb Breaking strain with around a meter of 8lb b/s fluorocarbon as leader material. Keeping it simple to start off. All methods work in different situations and different times of the year. The fun part is when you find the right combination of method/lure/colour etc on the day. Jig Heads/dropshot/spinners/cranks/spoons/vib/blade baits perch love them all but, the number one best for catching perch is a big juicy lobworm. A good set of forceps is a definite must have piece of equipment when using worms as bait as they will swallow it right down so forceps or a decent hook disgorger are necessary for retrieving the hook.

I'm lucky enough that my work involves a lot of travelling and I always have my perch tackle in the car in case of an emergency. With a bit of Google research the night before I would pick a couple of spots to try on my return trip providing I get my work finished and I can get an hour or three fishing. Being able to do this doesn't just make going to work at stupid o clock bearable but ultimately very enjoyable. I'm sure there are a few more people out there like me. I've found some fantastic fishing spots on my travels that I otherwise would never have visited only that I would be passing them on my way back home from work.

When trying new venues I always carry two rods. One for worms and the other for lures I've been on spots when the perch wouldn't look at a lure but would readily take the worm. I approach it like this as it's the best way to find if the perch are there or not. Also, on the lure rod if I'm dropshotting, instead of the dropshot regular weight I tie on a jig head so two different lures working different depths. I think that sometimes the two lures fishing together can really get the perch activated some days it really gets them on the take. Heavy vibe/blade baits can work well on the bottom end of the dropshot rig and of course the pike like them too so it results in an odd bite off if using fluorocarbon. I recommend a short light wire trace on the bottom of the dropshot so as to avoid the bite offs. Most pike that take the dropshot lure are lip hooked and I rarely get bitten off. When the pike take the dropshot lure, the leader from the top and bottom gets pushed away with the pikes mouth and stops the lure being inhaled. The pike move more delicately to the dropshot as its being fished, much slower than conventional lure tactics when they'll make a big lunge at the bait to stop it escaping. Sometimes this method results in a double hook up Double trouble or double the fun. You decide. I've had a couple of two pounders on at the same time and it does get a bit messy trying to land them. If you catch a few on the worm then you can switch to lures as it's always more fun. For instance, one venue I tried a few lures, nothing, try a worm = perch happy days. Switch rods back to lures = nothing, Switch back to worm = perch and so it went with no result on lures and all was caught on worms. If I hadn't caught on a worm I probably would not return to that area but I do now whenever I'm around the area, and yes I've since caught them on lures in that spot on different days.

One of my best lure days from the bankside resulted in 11 large perch with half of them just over the 40cms and 2lb+ and the rest were also from 1.5lb to 2lb. Absolute mayhem, although it is usually whilst fishing from a boat that results in the really big numbers of decent sized perch. The odd big one does show up from time to time. Some days you could catch them all day long on the big Loughs in Ireland. The dropshot is probably the best method once a shoal is located. It's the best way to keep your lure rig where the fish are. Some days they'll only take a virtually static lure and other days with a heavier dropshot weight and some really aggressive jerking is the only way to get a bite. I had a real eye opener while stewarding Team England at the world boat championships on Rutland water in 2018. It being their home water they knew what they were doing and I was amazed when for most of their fishing they were using heavy metal sea jigs of 20-30 gram and jigging them up and down the very same as jigging for mackerel at sea. I was more amazed when they started catching perch but their end result was pretty poor considering it was their home water. I think they finished 15th place out of 16 countries. Team Ireland finished a respectable 8th I think. Team England, the poor sods, thought they had won before it even started. A bit of an eye opener for them too. I'm definitely going to try that method on the big Loughs this year coming as I've already bought a few of the same heavy metal sea jigs.

A nice brace of perch.

Another thing to remember when lure fishing is that the perch will be inactive and seemingly oblivious to all going on around them. Just sitting on or near the bottom. They need activating. At these times it's worth trying a big bright lure that has lots of action and causes disturbance in the water. Cast it around the clock with aggressive jerking so that anything in the swim cannot miss the disturbance. Now, you may catch while doing this as it can work well on some days but it will definitely make the fish sit up and take notice. Of course, then if activated and maybe moving a little they probably think they're feeding. Then try switching back to smaller lures or dropshot and hopefully get some activated fish to take. Of course it doesn't always work but sometimes it does.

In the depths of winter when the water temperatures are way down, the Perch will be reluctant to chase down a fast moving lure, so, slowing the presentation right down to leaving it sitting on the bottom, stationary and inching it along and pause keeping touch, and inching and pause followed by some aggressive sharp jerks, let the lure settle and repeat. For me it's always after the sharp jerks when falling back to settle on the bottom is when I get most hits.

Another retrieve when mono comes into use as it sinks more easily than braid. When the jighead hits bottom, tighten up so as to sink the mono with the rod pointed down low. When you feel happy the mono is as straight to the lure as possible then try the very slowest retrieve of a light jig head with paddle tail or similar lure just enough to barely scrape the bottom mud. Watch the rod tip for anything like a slight bend as that is the take you won't feel because of the stretch properties of monofilament line. Any slight bend of the tip is the time to sweep the rod away to set the hook. It's amazing the difference this kind of retrieve makes when the perch are inactive. The new ultrafine braids are good too for this method but I find the monofilament better for its more neutral density creating less of a bow in the line once tightened to the lure and for finer presentations when the perch are being awkward. Effectively giving a more horizontal presentation and I think it works well on pressured perch as they are so accustomed to lures always being pulled upwards that this slight difference can put an extra few fish in the net on difficult days.

In my experience I find that when the air temperatures get to below 5 degrees Celsius for a long period the coldness completely kills the fishing. And the longer the cold snap the harder it will be to catch any fish. Now of course at some time of the day fish will feed but these feeding times are so short and being in the right place at the right time on these cold days is a bit of a lottery. But, there is light at the end of the tunnel because I know 100% fact that after a long cold spell (less than 5 degrees air temperature) when the temperatures rise up to between 5 and 10 degrees for a few days or maybe for a week long period the fish will make the most of the warmer weather and feed up before the next cold snap puts them back into a dormant state. This is the time you need to be on the water. I've had some amazing catches watching the rise in temperatures. It normally takes two or three days of higher temperatures for the feeding to take off but when it does I promise you some of the best fishing available on your local water. I've seen it year after year when the dreaded cold snaps arrive and completely kill the fishing. It could last a month or a fortnight but keep checking the weather reports and when you see the big rise in temperatures after the long cold snap it's time to cancel everything else and get the tackle ready. Honestly it's bonanza time. After one particular cold snap in January one year that lasted weeks the temperatures shot up to over 10 degrees and when I went pike fishing it seemed like every pike in the lake were on the rampage, almost every time I cast a bait there was a pike on it and I ended up with 28 pike and the biggest went 28lb 4oz. I know you've read it all in books before but it's such an actual real life happening prediction, too good to miss for anyone into their angling.

During the actual cold snaps (below 5 air temperatures) I use my light lure rods to ledger worms on a very simple but effective set up. A no.6 hook of light gauge on an 8lb b/s fluorocarbon leader and as little weight possible to get it to sit stationary on the river bed or canal or wherever you're fishing. It's important to keep the rod and line tight to the weight like feeder fishing without a feeder. This is so that bites will register on the rod tip as soon as there's any movement. Now, the most important part of this rig is the worm or two worms. Inject them with air which makes them pop up out of the bottom dirt and more visible to any passing fish. (that's where the light gauge hook comes into play as some hooks are just too heavy metal for presenting the worm like this) You'll need a very fine point needle and syringe for this and can be bought in chemists. Also if you think about ledgering worms normally. Say two lovely juicy lively dendrobaenas on a size 6 hook on the bottom silt. What do worms do only bury themselves into the mud. They need air to float off the bottom and you can rest assured that your bait is sitting pretty waiting to get chomped. It's not a new idea but when I first tried popping up worms it was on the river Boyne fishing for salmon before worms were banned. I know it's hard to believe that the oldest/bestest/bait in the world is now a criminal offence if you get caught using a worm on your local river. For goodness sake lads. Sorry, it's annoying, the worm ban thing. What a time to be alive. Izaak Walton must be spinning in his grave. I must agree with him about using worms as bait. One of the great piscator's phrases on using worms from the original book *"use him as though you loved him, that is, harm him as little as you may possibly, that he may live the longer."*

Popped worms for salmon were working brilliantly during high summer and low water levels when conventional salmon tactics were failing miserably. I was still pulling an odd fish from the river Boyne. (When reference is made to a fish on the river Boyne, it actually should be interpreted as a salmon, all other fish are referred to by their proper names, i.e. perch, roach etc but, a fish is a salmon).

Hard to beat a big perch.

MY FIRST 20LB+ PIKE
THE STRUGGLE IS REAL

Recaptures are inevitable especially on small lakes but it's a good feeling to meet up with old friends maybe months later or even the following season. One big pike wouldn't leave us alone during one seasons piking (October to March), she showed up 5 times on our rods and God only knows if anyone else had caught her. At the time, I still hadn't bagged the elusive 20 but came agonisingly close too many times. A few going 19lb 8oz and one even weighing 19lb 15oz but no cigar for that one. I had reliable information that I was on the right venue to break the 20lb barrier and it had become a major hurdle for me. That pike that we caught five times was instantly recognisable, a real old warrior probably on her last fling, she had many battle scars even from the first time I caught her. She had a spoon shaped dent in the top of her mouth and earned the name Lippy because of her regular appearances. I caught her 3 times. Once at 18lb then a month later, 19lb 8oz and post spawning 19lb 8oz. However I had my then piking accomplice, Danny, with me. Guess who shows up on his rod weighing 21lb? Yes, Lippy. Now, I was feeling some very strange fishing emotions, still 20 less. I'm guessing these fishing emotions don't even have names or have ever been categorized and most definitely never experienced by non fishing types. Feelings that only anglers, sharing boats with friends and relatives would understand. But, through gritted teeth I would always admire the capture of a 20lb plus pike.

My first 20+ pike at 22lb.

I had my older brother, Paul, with me on another day about a week later. He was bank fishing and I was in the dinghy. He phoned me to come and take a photo. When he opened the keepsack I said 21lb and he gave me a funny look. Of course it was Lippy again at 21lb. This was his 1st 20lb plus pike, in his lifetime spent fishing.

During this season I built a 13ft sailing skiff off plan, not for sailing of course, but to help with my quest for a 20lb plus pike. As luck would have it I was definitely fishing the right venues as my mates had 5 x 20lb pulse pike on board my boat before I finally managed to land one that weighed just over 22lbs on my homebuilt boat. They all said that it was a lucky boat but the luck took a long time to come around to my end of the boat and that's the strange thing about boat fishing. Fishing practically the same piece of water there are days when only one end of the boat will get all the action much to the annoyance of the person at the other end, but this definitely does happen with no obvious reason. Even using identical methods this is still possible. Don't even mention swapping places to opposite ends of the boat. Tempting fate too much even thinking about that one. I did let out a bit of a scream of relief when I finally caught my first 20lb+ pike after six seasons of watching my mates and relatives (some experienced and some novices too) catching all the 20s on my chosen venues. All the hard work and research was starting to pay off. This was in the early 2000s before social media kicked off and the only big pike I had seen in the whole of my many years of fishing were these ones that we had caught ourselves, which was something of an achievement at the time. Of course there were books and magazines etc with 20lb pike but to actually catch them was very rewarding as I was beginning to question if they were becoming a thing of the past. Thankfully from that first twenty onwards the big pike were coming like buses. I even have three over the magic 30 up to 34lb 10oz. Some day hopefully a 35lb plus pike will come my way. My second 20 as luck would have it was the same fish as my 1st 20. Having returned to the same venue, area a few weeks later I now had a second 20 also weighing 22lb and yes the photos confirmed that it was the same pike.

Messing about in boats with Caroline, Tommy and Abygail.

BATHTUB PIKE

A friend took his 8 year old son to a local lake for a bit of piking, as you do when you're left at home minding the kids! *'Yaay, let's go fishing, sure what else would you be doing.'* They weren't there long and the weather took a turn for the worse. Deciding to pack up early a big pike took the young fellas bait while he was reeling it in and they eventually landed the 18lb pike. The young fella was so impressed with his catch that he wanted to bring it home to show his mammy what a great angler he was. Instinct laying claim to alpha male dominance maybe. We're all animals at the end of the day. The Father of course wanted to release the pike but the insistent little fella got his way as they do and they wrapped the pike in a wet towel and put it in the boot of the car and hurried home. They filled the bath tub in the upstairs bathroom and put the pike in it.

On the mother's arrival home from work, the young fella was very excited. They rushed up to the bathroom, opened the door and flicked the light switch on and the pike shot up out of the bath and over their heads onto the landing and all kinds of messing about followed. It's such a bizarre story it must be true as you couldn't make it up if you tried, I believe the pike was released into the local canal the following morning and before the pike police start, this all happened back in the 1980, when pike appeared much more hardy than the snowflake pike of today.

BIG PIKE, SMALL LAKES

By big pike, I mean pike that are over 20lb in weight. Almost all of my big pike are from small lakes in the northeast counties of Ireland. Living within an hour's drive of most of them is the main reason for fishing this area and it takes time to unlock the secrets of any venue, so less driving means more fishing time. In my opinion, a good percentage of these lakes will hold maybe a couple of big pike, though this may not become apparent for a long time. It may take years of fishing some lakes, before getting or even seeing a big girl. Nobody said it was going to be easy and a little friendly sharing of local information can reduce the time and effort involved. So, be nice to others that you meet on your chosen venues. Just recently a 28lb+ pike was caught in a small lake that has been hammered since pike fishing was invented circa 1984. The same lake had also taken a bad hammering from our foreign visitors who like to eat pike. Then in 2016 out comes a 28lb pike. I had scarcely heard of even a low double coming out of it before.

Over the years I've noticed this happening on a few small Jack lakes I'll call them, then boom, out comes a monster pike. If it's a big pike that you're after then you should only concentrate on the lakes that you know from a 100% reliable source or actually witnessed a big one being caught from. Two or three lakes would be enough to concentrate on for the winter season. I might add here that to my knowledge all of these lakes go completely dead for pike during the summer months. Believe me I've tried enough of them in the summer and it's almost impossible to catch any pike let alone a big one. October is a good time to start your campaign, and stick with the chosen lakes right through the winter pike season until you know that they've finished spawning which is usually in March. I normally finish fishing these lakes in mid March as after spawning they go dormant for a while, maybe a few weeks when again it's hard to catch even a few juvenile pike.

It may be worth concentrating on one venue for the whole of the season if you know for sure that it holds a big pike. So, for five months from October to March, if you were to fish one day a week which is what normal working people can realistically manage, then twenty days is the time frame you have to work with. Other factors come into play like flooding, or even worse, iced over lakes can knock days off your limited time. This is when you need a backup river venue.

In my personal experience, it's better to stick it out on the one venue for the duration and you'll eventually come across the bigger fish. It's just a matter of you and them crossing paths. Stick it out until the end of the season and expect the dreaded blank sessions. February being the best chance of a big girl, then January 2nd best, then December 3rd best. It's possible to get a lucky big fish at any time, but my diaries show that sequence of big pike captures being best in February, being full of spawn of course can add up to a fifth of the overall weight of the pike, then weight added from feeding up all adds up.

One pike I caught on St. Stephen's day at 25lb 9oz reappeared on March 1st, this time at a whopping 29lb. She was full of spawn and I could feel a large lump in her gut, I'm guessing bream, possibly near a pound in weight. A massive 3lb 7oz weight gain in two months. Not many big pike were showing up back then or is it social media that's bringing bigger pike to our attention than before? I made the front cover of the then popular monthly magazine *'Irish Anglers Digest.'* A very proud moment for me, back when actual printed magazines were the norm.

I think everyone loved the actual printed magazines of the day. Always trying to get to the newsagent on release day in case they were sold out. It would be put to one side so you could enjoy it at your leisure with a nice cuppa and a bikky maybe.

29lb pike that made the front cover of Irish Anglers Digest.

If it's possible for you to fish your chosen venue in February, this will definitely increase your chance of that special fish of a lifetime. My PB pike at 34lb10oz was caught in February. Unfortunately, I couldn't get a great photo of it as it was getting dark and I was on a solo session. Consulting my diary it was another uneventful day and I had dropped two large popped roach with the bait boat over 100 meters from the shore. Towards the end of the day, I dropped them a second time about 70-80 meters out which resulted in the only bite for the day, but it was the one I was waiting for. Sometimes people would ask, how long did it take you to catch it? All my life is the answer.

34lb 10oz P.B. as the light was fading.

YOU NEVER KNOW

You never really know for sure what's going on under water. Part of the fun of fishing I guess. On one occasion at a pike bank competition on Lough Gowna the water was as clear as crystal. I could see large bream in the margins in the middle of spawning. I had caught a couple of jacks and bites were hard to come by. Casting my 6 inch albino line through trout I could clearly see it coming through the water a good distance from where I stood. Watching the lure I was amazed when a pike of around 6lbs took it, shook it, and spat it out in the blink of an eye. Nothing registered either on the line or the rod and I didn't feel the slightest thing. If I hadn't seen it I would never have known I actually had a bite. Normally you would feel the bite first. How many times does this happen during a day's fishing? There are some things in life that we'll never know. A few more casts and no show from the pike. I fished along the margins for a while and returned to the same spot with a different lure. A jerkbait. I made the same cast as when I had seen the pike earlier, and watching the jerkbait coming through the water on the same spot, the same pike I guess, took the lure, shook it, and spat it out and again no bite registering anywhere on the line, the rod or the feel of the thud normally felt when lure fishing. I went about my business trying to catch whatever I could but it was one of those days when the pike were ignoring me. A few hours later returning to the same spot, this time I had a smelt dead bait on and covered the same spot again, watching the wobbling smelt coming slowly through the water and there was the pike swimming about an inch behind it, tracking it. I'll just add here that if a fish is following a lure or bait I think its a normal reaction to stop the bait to let the fish get it but this nearly always puts the fish off and if anything it's probably better to speed it up a little and induce a take. The pike followed my bait about an inch behind all the way into about a foot of water and I had to stop reeling under the rod tip. The smelt settled on the bottom. The pike lay still for about ten seconds, turned slowly and swam away.

Coincidentally around that time I came across a conversation on an online forum about bites not registering on rods etc. One person's waterwolf recording of three hours trolling that day when he caught nothing, revealed that no less than twelve pike had taken his lures and not even one of the takes registered on the rod. Another person in that conversation was trolling for trout all day and caught two trout on a quiet day. On checking the water wolf recording it revealed a shoal of up to fifty trout following his lures at different points during the day. You just never know.

INFLATABLE FUN

In an ideal situation one would be able to juggle working days, family commitments and home life and fishing days could be switched to suit the better weather days. Wind is a big consideration, especially if you a on an 8ft rubber dinghy or worse still, a float tube. I've never tried a float tube and don't intend to as they look like hard work and having my feet dangling in the icy cold water all winter does not appeal to me in any way, shape, or form, but each to their own devices. I've spent enough days in the dingy, above the water level, freezing my nuts off to know that feet dangling in the water all day cannot be a good thing. The rubber dinghy is a great way of tackling these small lakes and makes an ideal fishing platform or even for dropping baits at distance on the windy days when it's not safe to be afloat. Believe me, it's much more preferable than trudging around the margins in the mud, with drains, fences, dykes and swamps that are characteristic of most of these small lakes that are actually worth the effort. Chuck all you need for the day into the dingy and away you go. One tactic I use regularly to cover as much water as possible, drop a lightly weighted popped up dead bait off the dinghy and drive the dinghy 150 meters or so onto the margins, usually rushes, and drop anchor. Then work the dead bait back slowly towards myself, pausing, maybe every 10 meters or so. I find that the longer the bait is left sitting, it increases the bite possibility of a take. Also, depending on wind direction I would have dropped a second bait on a large (Hi-viz) float at the same distance. Of course the floated bait will need to be on the downwind side depending which direction is blowing. If there's a nice breeze the floating braid will be towing along with the wind at a nice pace. The floating braid being perfect for catching the surface wave and dragging the float around in an arc, presenting the dead bait nice and slow across the bay area. Two floated baits will tend to result in tangles, so that's why the other bait is lightly ledgered (with just enough weight to keep the popped bait on the bottom) Mend the arc from time to time so as not to have too much slack line out. Vast areas of water can be covered with these tactics while safely tucked into the margins somewhere out of the wind and rain. If I'm not getting any action, on the days when the pike are inactive, then it's time for the doughnut manoeuvre. Honestly, try it, it does work and very well some days if you get it right. This is a great way of covering large shallow bays and I've had some of my best days and biggest pike using these tactics.

Fishing regularly on a particular lake will enable you to understand the lakes moods regarding wind and temperatures, etc.

It's not easy by any stretch of the imagination and it takes a certain amount of dedication to sit out in a dinghy in north westerly gale force winds, but if it's your only day off that week I think you'll understand that it's all part of the fun. Another word to describe it might be Lunacy. If you have put in another full day with not much to show, on your own and barely able to feel your hands and feet with the cold you will definitely begin to question your own sanity. It's like being one of the great explorers or the great white hunter. Much more fun experiencing actual severe weather than sitting at home and looking at it on a screen. When you do get home possibly with a nice photo of your new PB pike. It's time to pop a nice bottle of red and celebrate. That one pike that will up the PB makes it all worthwhile. But hey, you could be doing a lot worse things like sitting in a pub or a bookies for the day. I even had two days when I had two 20lb+ pike. That's the buzz, and straight away I'm thinking could I make it three. I'm still dreaming of that one! Maybe one day when the stars align. Like I said these small lakes will only hold a few big pike unlike the Big Loughs of Ireland that can produce great numbers of big pike 20lb+ for those in the know. Strangely though very few over the 30lb barrier are revealed from the big Loughs. The big Loughs are a different entity and a different set of methods required to unlock their secrets. I personally don't have enough experience on this type of venue so I'll leave them to the experts, for now.

PIKE – Dead baiting

As I sit here on my first dead baiting session of the year, looking at a blank card with only two hours of daylight left, it's not looking good, but, the dead baiter that's after only big pike learns that blanking is better than having your large best-presented bait being constantly mangled by jacks. If your bait is being taken by jacks, then it cuts down on your fishing time, having to re-bait, and unhooking jacks etc is all eating into your time of having your big bait in the water, waiting for the one big pike. I am a firm believer in using the biggest dead baits, probably up to 12oz in weight. I can almost hear the laughing, *"Big? You call that big?"* My mate uses 2lb bream as dead bait, and bigger if he can get it. I'm still waiting to actually see anyone using bigger baits than me. My number one choice would be a big roach or a hybrid. I get most of my big baits from Lough Neagh commercial eel fishers, and the big roach/hybrids are a by/catch from the eel fishing. I like to pop up my big baits. Various different options are available in fishing tackle shops. I use the foam hair curlers that are cheap and readily available in chemists and euro budget shops. They're made of foam with a wire running through the middle that already has a wire loop on either end, which makes them ideal for attaching to your trace wire with either trace wire or mono. Sometimes, I catch hard on the bottom but the way I see it is that your bait could be lying out of sight in the dirt so I feel more confident with the baits popped up, knowing that they'll be more visible to any passing pike plus the bigger sized bait generally keeps the jack pike away and usually when you do get a run it'll result in at least a low double figure pike (over 10lb in weight) Not always of course. Or, are all of the smaller pike avoiding the general area for fear of being gobbled up by Big mama. Some things we will never know for sure, except for the fact that when you think you have it 100% figured out the pike will go and change the rules, again.

To avoid deep hooking I always hook my big deadbait with the head facing up the trace (wobbling style). It's only on a very rare occasion that I get a deep hooked pike. Even with a deep hooked one, the hooks will still be visible and are relatively easy to remove. As we all know the pike turns the bait to swallow it head first. So, head first in the mouth means that the hook points are pointing towards the throat inside the pike's mouth. As the pike is trying to swallow the bait some of the hooks on the two trebles will get snagged somewhere on the way through the mouth area. Sometimes the hooks may even catch on the outside of the mouth and this will probably result in a dropped run. If the bait is hooked in the usual fashion with the head facing down the trace the hooks will have no resistance and can slide freely down into the gut which we definitely do not want to happen. Of course conventional bolt rigs work very well but I personally don't like using heavy weights for static deadbaiting as most of the lakes I fish on have soft muddy or silty bottoms. The heavier weight can sink into the mud pulling the bait down, especially when tightening up to the weight for proper bite indication it can pull the weight deeper into the mud. With the bait hooked head up (wobbling style) the hooks pointing towards the throat will catch somewhere on all the nooks and crannies in the pike mouth and when the pike feels this, it will panic and take off at speed (bolt) so it's just a matter of tightening up and a swift lift of the rod to set the hooks properly. There are many different theories on the subject of bold rigs and I've tried and tested my version over many years and only very rarely have the hooks made it to the top of the throat area and would still be visible and relatively easy to retrieve.

I am on the spot (while writing this) that produced my personal best 34lb 10oz earlier this same year and also a 32lb 12oz pike the previous season. These fish are absolute monsters and have to be seen in the flesh to appreciate how magnificent a creature they are. There are plenty of other good swims on this particular lake that could produce a steady catch of decent pike but I've caught enough of them in the past so happy to suffer the blank sessions waiting for a hungry mama to cross paths with me. I also find bait boats invaluable in my dead baiting sessions, for achieving greater distances but more importantly for bait presentation. For instance, try casting a 12oz roach more than 40 or 50 meters. Even with proper rigging, bait elastic etc the baits just don't look as natural plus the hooks are going to pull through the flesh and tear it. Then, when the bait smashes down onto the surface of the water the look will be a lot less natural from the damage occurring during the pressure of casting and landing hard on the water. With the bait boat, I can keep the whole rig very simple with nothing more than two trebles on a 30lb B/S wire trace lightly hooking the bait. The bait then gently falls to the bottom with some weight fixed to the upper trace and sits perfectly naturally looking and pops off the bottom. How can the poor pike resist? At this point I'd just like to say that for me luck never entered the equation when I crossed paths with these magnificent beasts. Being in my 50's now I have dedicated the last twenty years trying to track these leviathans down. So, be prepared for the long haul friends. Of course, you might be lucky and first cast Boom, a 35lber. It has happened and when this happens that's usually an end to the pursuit of big pike, as where do you go from there? Sometimes the chase is better than the catch. Being sent the wrong road, lake, river etc by others in the search of the beasts is all part and parcel of the world of pike fishing. There are a lot of cloak and dagger shenanigans in the pursuit of big pike. However, it's all part of the fun and I've been at both ends of the playing field on many occasions. So, this session finished without a run and due to work commitments and being generally kept busy I missed my opportunity and sure enough, someone bagged a fine 37lb fish from the very same swim that season. Now the word is out I rarely get a chance on that swim anymore, and of course, it's not producing with the extra pressure. I'm hoping they'll (the anglers) will eventually move off after a few more blanks. The pain is very real, believe me.

A 30 lb plus on the dead bait.

THE GETAWAY BOAT

My new 15hp Yamaha 4 stroke outboard was stolen from the back of my beloved Orkney 14ft Coastliner. Parked outside my living room window and us asleep in the bed room directly above. We didn't hear a thing despite the fact that the thieves had to unbolt it, and cut steering cables etc. Even my little dog, Skipper, that used to bark at everything didn't bark. The insurance covered most of the cost but I was reluctant to replace the engine in case it would happen again. I left the engineless boat in Shercock, Cavan, where we had a mobile holiday home on the banks of Lough Sillan while thinking about getting a new engine.

Occasionally I would take the Orkney out with the little electric trolling motor when the weather was suitable. One such day I arrived at the mobile site and was surprised that my friend Ken, had his boat at the opposite side of the lake. Ken rarely ever used the boat and it was usually half full of water. It was a similar style of boat to the Orkney and was tied up at one of the jetties at the mobile park. There was no sign of Ken or his car or anyone else for that matter as it was in the depths of winter and no one used the mobile homes this time of year. I had just launched my boat and Ken arrived and we were both baffled as to how the boat broke its moorings. There had been a fierce storm the day before but we didn't think that was the reason. I went to recover Ken's boat using the electric trolling motor and was surprised to find that it was securely tied up to a tree in bank side vegetation overhanging the water. A totally unsuitable place to disembark from a boat. The boat was full to the gunnels with water but still afloat so I slowly towed it back over to where Ken was waiting (about half a kilometre across) By the time I made the short trip the sites caretaker Ollie had arrived on the scene.

Ollie was to reveal a remarkable account of how Ken's boat was on the opposite side of the lake.

Two members of An Garda Siochana (Ireland's Police force) were transporting a convicted murderer from an appeal hearing back to prison some distance away in the next county. Allegedly the young man had murdered his mother some years previously. On their way the Garda decided to stop at a filling station (about a kilometre away) on the outskirts of Shercock village for a cup of tea. I'm imagining a scene straight out of the TV series Father Ted. At some point the convict absconded and ended up in the mobile park. Luckily there was no one around during the winter period. Kens boat was the only boat left out on the jetties and had a pair of oars in it and off the convict went rowing like a lunatic in the middle of the storm. Obviously a desperate man with nothing to lose. The Garda were waiting for him on the opposite side when he finally got through the scrub and the trees. I can only imagine the job they had in the mucky fields trying to apprehend this desperate madman, but they did eventually after a long struggle. I guess stories like this are never reported for a reason. You couldn't make it up as they say. Ken took a new sense of pride in the old boat as it was now known as the getaway boat with a good story attached to it, and we all love a good story.

PIKE... BOAT FISHING (Tournaments)

Generally when pike fishing from a boat, I will cast or troll lures. I don't like trolling much and only troll as a last resort on days when I couldn't buy a bite for love nor money. One top tip on the really tough days is Doughnuts. Honestly, If you are in an area that you know usually holds pike and you've been through every lure in the box twice over, depending on depth, knock your big outboard into gear and drive around the area in a tight circle, maybe 30 or 40 meters diameter. Do these slow doughnuts two or three times even through lily pads etc. Then cut the engine and start casting in and around the area you've circled. You might be pleasantly surprised that it actually does work. The fish are there but inactive so the engine and boat disturbance basically stirs up the soup and they wake up and start moving or at the very least looking up at your lures passing over and hopefully making a go at them. This manoeuvre I'm going to coin as the doughnut manoeuvre. This has saved the day for me on a number of occasions even in competitions and helped to secure top rankings in major events on more than one occasion. In the shallower water slow is better but in deeper water after picking up some large shapes on the fish finder whizzing around at a much faster speed can get the fish moving off bottom. Generally speaking if fish are showing on screen tight on the bottom you'll struggle to catch them but if they're anywhere off the bottom you've a better chance of a take.

On one occasion at a boat competition, a qualifying heat for the World boat championships, I was paired up with a new boat partner, Mark Flynn, from Dublin, and we were struggling to catch at all. I was driving, so I suggested the doughnut manoeuvre, my boat partner and the steward, who was on board to measure and record catches, were looking at me as if I was totally bonkers. To be honest I'm always surprised when it does work myself, but it definitely does. Like I said we did manage to boat a few pike securing us a second place in one of the qualifying heats for the world championships. They probably still think I'm bonkers though. Another trick is to cast into the wash of any passing boats as this also stirs the pike up and an odd bonus fish can be added to the scoreboard. .

On the subject of the World Lure boat championships, I eventually teamed up with good friend Simon Gibson and together we successfully qualified to represent Ireland at the world championships on three occasions so far. Another one of note was winning the Dragon Masters boat event for which we received a 17ft fibreglass built boat and 1500 euro worth of fishing tackle. Both myself and Simon individually making the shore team on a number of occasions The boat qualifying heats organised by the NCFFI are usually four full days of intense competition on the big Loughs in Ireland, Lough Ree, Lough Derg, and the upper and lower Lough Erne systems. I absolutely love taking part in the qualifiers and anyone that's interested in entering please contact me through social media and I'll do my very best to help you get started. Being on a two man team for the boat qualifiers requires 100% dedication, commitment and effort. Under no circumstances can you ever give less than 100% effort. With both of us having our respective tasks at either end of the boat and also putting in a lot of days travelling and practicing on competition venues before the main event. This takes an awful lot of time and effort not to mention the costs involved, days booked off work etc. So, like I said 100% commitment before you even cast a lure.

On another occasion at an IFPAC bank competition on the Shannon, I won the competition with about 40lb of pike. The fishing was difficult that day and not much was being caught. I was floating a small roach across and downstream in a narrow part of the river that normally would hold a few pike. Around midday the boat/cruiser traffic started to pick up. As the 1st boat approached there was plenty of clearance from my floated offering so I left it to drift. As the boat passed the float disappeared, fish landed, weighed and released, happy days. So it went, another cruiser passing and the float went under. Another pike to weigh and release. Amazingly this happened seven times one after the next, every time a cruiser passed the float went under and I finished 1st with over 40lb of pike out of approximately 80 anglers. I know it sounds hard to believe but I still find that kind of stuff pretty amazing and always worth a try on a difficult day.

The IFPAC, The Irish federation of Pike Angling Clubs, also have an annual All Ireland Inter club event which attracts huge interest from affiliated pike clubs from every corner of our beautiful island. Up to 32 teams of 4 anglers taking part in a catch and release pike event. Each club can enter as many teams as they like and fishing is normally for five hours with one member of each team fishing in one of the four lakes chosen for the competition. It's a highly coveted title and very competitive. Our team Drogheda & District Anglers Club, were to win it twice in 2010 and 2012 when I guess we were at the top of our game, the glory years.

CAROLINE'S PIKE

During the year 2020, myself and my wife Caroline made great use of our little 14ft Orkney Coastliner with the 25 HP Outboard to push her along. We had many camping /boating trips any time the Covid-19 travel restrictions were lifted. We were truly blessed with the weather during that Summer. On one of these camping trips to Lough Ree, the weather was simply as good as it ever gets in Ireland and we joyfully motored around the Lough and the river Shannon. Every day we would bring a picnic, some beer and wine for our days out. It was never terribly difficult to catch a few decent sized perch and pike and, of course that would keep me interested, while Caroline would read a book or magazine.

With the weather being so pleasant I remember thinking that I could not be in a better place, everything is as it should be and we were both healthy and happy and still in love after all these years. Both in our 50's, and still in steady employment, a beautiful daughter and son now in their early 20's and our mortgage paid off. While drifting around on the Lough in the beautiful sunshine and light breeze, all of these thoughts came flooding into my mind at the same time and I experienced a wonderful euphoric feeling, with the realisation of how good life actually is. If there was a point in time that it was ever possible to return to, then that would be it. Sheer happiness. Time to relax.

On one of our trips down the Shannon, I dropped Caroline off at the main bridge that crosses the Shannon in Athlone. She went and got some provisions for the barbecue that we were planning that evening. I stayed with the boat while she was shopping, and easily caught some perch and a nice Jack in and around the marina.

When I collected Caroline (The boat taxi) we realised that she had forgotten the burger buns for the planned barbecue later that evening So, I tied up at the marina and went off to get some and Caroline stayed with the boat to read her book in the beautiful sunshine.

I had left my three lures rods in the rod rack with the lures hooked onto the bottom eye on each rod as is usual. On my return I was walking down the jetty and noticed Caroline with one of the rods and thought *'ahh that's nice, she's finally starting to like fishing.'* When she saw me coming she started shouting, *"hurry up, hurry up will you? It's a big one."* Of course I thought she was messing around and didn't hurry at all. She kept on shouting to hurry and I said *"yeah yeah"* as I imagined the bend in the rod was probably a bottle of water or something that she had tied to the end of the line as a joke for a laugh. As I calmly stepped onto the boat she handed the rod to me and boy was I surprised as at the end of the line was an angry pike around 10lb in weight. After landing the pike and a quick photo and release I was congratulating Caroline on her angling skills, hooking such a lovely pike on a lure. Well, I'm not sure how it happened but she swore blind that she never casted the rod, but just saw it slipping over the side of the boat and grabbed hold of it and the pike was already attached. Of course I didn't believe her. The rod didn't cast itself, or did it? After much deliberation we finally pieced together how this very strange turn of events might have happened. This is what we think might have happened. There was a good flow in the river and the water was crystal clear. So, some gentle movement on the boat had somehow tilted the rod loosely in the rod rack, and also the lure (a professor spoon) had somehow unhooked from the bottom eye on the rod and would have been barely under the surface of the water. We tested our theory as to how this could possibly happen and there was enough line from the rod tip to the lure for it to dangle just under the surface and sure enough the spoon was turning slowly and flashing in the current. I'm still amazed that the pike, especially a marina pike that's probably seen more lures than me, actually snaffled the spoon, right at the side of the boat. It's a far fetched tale but true. I'm still in awe of the strange turn of events that happened that day on the Shannon.

PIKE COMPETITIONS (Bank)

Some people like competitions and some don't for whatever reasons but I personally think they're great fun and open up a whole different level of angling opportunities. I've been competing at local level since I started fishing at a young age.

I'll try and relate my competition strategy as best I can and hopefully it'll benefit you in some small part. Starting as a teenager in local club competitions, without trying too hard I would often get a place in the top three in these competitions and sometimes even win one or two. It's a very rewarding feeling. Back then it was a lot more of a relaxed day out and not as competitive as it is by today's standards.

Preparing the night before a competition is an important factor for me. Making sure that every single piece of tackle is 100% exactly as you want it. Now is not the time to try out any new piece of equipment or new lures etc. I've seen this happen time and time again from others. Use your tried and tested tackle that you already know works well. Always, always, always keep your bait or lure in the water as much as is possible. (Obvious, I know) from the very first to the very last second of the match. Even when moving to different spots keep casting while walking the shoreline. A bonus fish picked up like this can be a game changer. It's funny the way the news travels around the venue that someone has caught a huge pike or two. Ignore these stories as best you can as they are not always true. You, after all are, competing with the fish and for the duration of the competition stay focused on your goal, catch as many fish as is possible for you on the day. Even if you don't get into the placings, it's all good practice for the next event. When you get back to the weigh in you might be pleasantly surprised when you find out that those one or two big pike you'd heard about were only rumours. Do your research of the venue before the event. Access points, terrain, weed beds, depths, adjoining rivers, drains, dykes, etc. This will save valuable time. If the area where you've chosen to start isn't producing any or very little fish for you or others then its best to leave that area, maybe even jump into the car and get to the other side of the lake. Fresh water that hasn't already been fished over can be a gamble but that's when you need a bit of luck. With the bank fishing you'll come across some almost impossible situations just to get your bait/lure fishing properly whether it be high rushes or floating weed/lily pads or having to wade sometimes up to your elbows deep in the margins. This all takes a lot of time and practice but that's all part of the fun. Working along the margins hopefully will find some feeding fish. If you do catch one it's definitely worth stopping in that area and giving it a good going over using all of your best tricks and tactics. Different fish may react to different methods, so keep juggling stuff around to get the fish interested. When I'm in this search mode I find it very hard to leave a bait sitting on the bottom and waiting for a fish to pick it up. Some days though it's the only way to get a much needed fish in the net. Floating a small nicely presented dead bait is my more favourable approach and there's nothing better than watching that float slide away and slowly diving under the surface. No need for a big sweep of the rod. Just reel down tightly until the rod starts to bend a little and a quick lift should set the hooks. Keep maximum pressure between your rod and the fish as sometimes the pike has clamped onto the bait and when you tighten up you're effectively pulling the pike towards you, so the hooks haven't actually moved in the pike's mouth, if the pike releases its grip, it's gone. It probably sounds strange but after happening a few times you'll understand it better.

Some days the pike will be inactive. If fishing an area you know would usually hold a few pike and the pike are not reacting to your efforts, try the biggest brightest jerkbait in your box, casting around the clock causing as much commotion and disturbance as possible. If you don't catch on the jerkbait, switch back to a small floated dead bait and take time to cover the same area and hopefully put an extra few fish in the net. This has worked for me on numerous occasions. I remember chatting with my brother Paul about the effects of causing disturbance in and on the water at one IFPAC competition. The fishing was difficult on that particular day and very few active pike were being caught. There was a reed bed in the middle of the river where Paul was fishing and I was about 100 meters upstream when I heard two huge splashes downriver where he was fishing. I was curious and looking down towards him and about a minute later I could see he was stuck into a big fish. I ran down and netted it – a 15lb+ pike. He explained the two splashes were two big stones as big as he could manage to lob into the reed bed in the middle of the river and the first cast resulted in the 15lb+ pike in the net which put him in the placings that day. There were a few more stones lobbed into rivers after that day. It's the interesting days like that which keep us going.

A one time P.B. 32lb 4oz.

EAST COAST

I'll start by letting you know the situation along the east coastline from Bettystown, Co Meath to Dundalk Bay off the Co Louth coast. This is, the closest bit of sea to where I live and has been totally overfished by commercials over a number of years. So much so that none of the local trawlers ever fish there. The only boats fishing this area are trawling razor fish from the sandy bottom, and a few lobster boats fishing over the rougher ground in the patches that aren't desert This involves dragging their fishing gear through the top layers of sandy ground covering every inch of coastline with this type of bottom structure. Day in day out 24/7 for most of the year, completely destroying everything in their path, not a blade of seaweed or much else survives this dredging. It sickens me that it was allowed to come to this. Honestly, the sea bed is like a sandy desert with no habitat for our native fish species. Mackerel are the only fish in abundance here when they visit us and that's during the summer months. We rarely even see a dogfish where most places can be plagued by them at times. The bass have survived as they inhabit the shallower coastline and can be found in decent sizes. Perhaps they feed around the Razor boats picking off the numerous other types of small shellfish that are disturbed with the dredging. Thousands of these small shellfish are washed up regularly on the local beaches, with shells sometimes covering the beaches in large drifts of dead empty shellfish shells. I don't think anyone in Ireland eats razor fish, they all go for export I expect. I believe the razor fish get a good price at the fish market. Chatting to a lad that works on the Razor boats as the tides get bigger, ie, the spring tides, it gives the razor boats an extra few meters where they can get closer to the shoreline so, even that last few meters that were left untouched on the neap tides (small tides) get destroyed. The relentless destruction of our coastline and fish/shellfish stocks. While I'm on the subject of our seas and oceans being destroyed for profit I would like to try and relate that it is of course the consumer that is the number one culprit in this scenario. Yes, you and I. Every time you or I buy a piece of fresh fish, even worse to buy frozen supermarket fish that are being constantly harvested and stored and let's not forget the canned fish that are being constantly processed and sitting for how long in storage. So, in my opinion, if you are buying fish. Buy fresh and leave all the frozen, canned fish on the shelves or even better to catch your own but only ever take enough for a meal or two. No stocking up your freezer please. Anyway, frozen fish will never taste as good as a fresh piece of fish so choose your species to suit the season.

TOPE

I own a 14 foot Orkney Coastliner with a 25hp mariner 2 stroke on the back. I have it for fifteen years now and it's a super little boat that's done everything asked of it and more. I've always felt completely safe at sea despite being caught in some rough weather at times. I'm going to keep her going as long as I can as it's so easy to launch and recover even single-handed and I have no need or desire to complicate the simple things in life. One minus is probably it's just a little bit on the small size for landing a big tope, but we still manage ok. Tope are an absolute beast of an animal. None of the other fish I mentioned in this book can come near to the complete savage nature of a tope. Honestly, until you've tried actually holding onto a tope just out of the water you wouldn't understand. I highly recommend every angler to try it someday as the sheer power of these sharks is hard to believe. Plus in a small boat like my one it kind of turns landing one into a kind of wrestling match or cage fighting with Conor McGregor, no doubt you'll come away with some bad body burns the first few times so be careful. I always wear long heavy-duty rubber gloves to avoid getting the wrist knuckle burn from wrestling with the tope. This happens when the topes skin rubs against yours like rough sandpaper and causes the ugliest dirty looking scabs imaginable. They can't be felt much at the time but gradually get dirtier looking for weeks afterwards, not nice.

Before the Mackerel arrive in big numbers is the best time to target Tope. From mid-May onwards right through the summer months until late October is the most productive time on the east coast of Ireland. Weather permitting of course. I would normally have some frozen mackerel saved from the previous season to use as bait but fresh mackerel flappers are without a doubt the best bait I have used. Even if you can only catch a few mackerel for bait it will greatly improve your chances of catching. When a Tope takes your bait, you will definitely know as normally the line screams off the reel at a ferocious speed. When this happens I've seen grown men turn back into little school kids in an instant and completely lose the run of themselves with the sheer excitement and panic that ensues. It must be seen to be believed, some of the coolest, hardest types of men completely melt into little children. It's a very unusually funny experience to behold, but all in good fun so everyone enjoys the ride that follows the screaming runs.

Spending all of my youthful summers with my parents in our caravan in Clogherhead, Co Louth, a small fishing village on the east coast of Ireland, the summers were timeless as are the memories from youth, and the weather was always fair, as our memories declare. I sometimes wonder if today's children will have such fond memories or are their poor minds too clogged up with today's technology. I do hope that's not the case though I fear it may be true. I spent many happy days clambering over the rocky headland, searching rock pools and fishing from the rocks and Clogherhead pier/harbour. Back then in the 70's and early 80's, it was still possible to catch decent Coalfish, Pollack, and Codling up to 4lb in weight. Also, an odd decent sized Plaice or Gurnard thrown into the mix, and always on very basic tackle as that's all we had back then. Of course, we knew most of the fish species and Tope were sharks that were caught in faraway places like deep sea charters over on the west coast of Ireland and such exotic locations.

Fast forward from 1980 to the year 2000. Having returned from making my fortune in London with my wife Caroline and 1st born Tommy, I bumped into an old friend I had made while on the building sites in London, Big Denis Coll, who had married a local girl from Drogheda. Big Den, a Donegal man that could never really settle anywhere for too long. But, a nicer man you could not meet and we had already shared a few adventures in London town. Den told me that during the previous week he met a man from Navan launching a small boat on the slipway at Clogher harbour and was going in search of Tope. Big Den was born in a boat and cannot resist any chance of being on the water or in it for that matter. Of course, he offered to accompany this fella going for Tope. My ears could hardly believe what I was hearing. He told me they caught two Tope around 20 or 30lbs. Never in my life had I heard of fish this size around Clogherhead. Big Den agreed to meet me the following morning at the slipway and we would go to the general area where they had caught. Off we went the next morning kitted out with some standard pike fishing gear. I must add here that Standard pike tackle is not recommended for Tope fishing. You might land a few lucky ones but the tope will definitely smash some part of the rig, be it the trace wire or swivels, crimps etc or even roll up onto the braid and braid is no match for tope skin. He was able to judge his bearings from the local landmarks and as it turned out we were definitely on a Tope mark. We were only about a mile off the shoreline and when I dropped the anchor I was very surprised that it was only about 20ft depth. I had to ask him was he sure about the spot as I was assuming some great depth of water was needed for big fish, but yes he said he was sure. My first cast and I had a baby one of around 4lb weight and not long after I was stuck into something more powerful than I had ever experienced in all my fishing life. Honestly, the reel was almost smoking with the line screaming off the drag on long powerful runs, my heart was in my mouth and I was probably screaming some expletives. Could I land this Monster from the deep? Yes, I could hardly believe what I was looking at from the side of the boat. A proper member of the shark family. This was the greatest fishing buzz I'd had in many years fishing, we went on to catch another one of 30lbs I was in fishing heaven that day catching sharks in my own boat in my local waters. No fish finders/chart plotters etc back then so just some good old school fishing. With no knowledge of tope and never having met one in the flesh, we managed to catch three up to 30lb in weight in a short session. Not knowing how to handle them properly I foolishly decided to weigh one of them in one of those triangular folding landing nets commonly used for salmon etc. I put the tope in the landing net and rested it on the deck. Big mistake as the Tope started rolling and the net handle was flying around like a propeller bashing everything in the boat including me and Big Den. Mayhem. By the time we got it under control, the landing net was completely demolished, the triangular arms and the main handle all broken in pieces with the actual net wrapped so tightly around the Tope that we had to cut the net to set the tope free. Vivid memories.

An average sized tope around 30lbs.

Well, that was the start of another new chapter in my fishing life and every year it's really something to look forward to once the weather settles during the month of May. It's usually possible to get a few fresh Mackerel even in the month of May but the Tope are less fussy at that time of year and can be caught on frozen herrings and mackerel. Fresh is best of course and to make a Maccy flapper basically means removing the backbone from the mackerel so you're left with a head and two fillets attached. the fresh flapper will release the best scent and blood particles once in the water and if there are tope about they usually cannot resist and gobble it down quickly, so don't leave them too long on the bite as if they swallow the hook there's no chance of unhooking them due to the razor-sharp shark teeth. Of course, it doesn't work every time we go tope fishing, but on average I guess it works more than 50% of the time.

Like all types of fishing, some days it's easy and some days it's hard to get a run. The average where I fish is around 30lbs and I've had them up to 60lbs. A friend of mine launches at the opposite side of Dundalk Bay and has had Tope weighting up to 78lbs and I've heard of Tope over 100lbs caught by commercial trawlers.

Chumming is any kind of fish parts or whole fish chopped and minced if possible and it can play a big part in improving your catch but not essential. Of course, if you have chum definitely get it down there. I use old onion sacks or similar netting and filled with chum attach it to the anchor. The downside of chumming is it'll attract every crab in the area and they'll destroy every bait you prepare unless a tope gets to it first. To avoid the crabs getting my bait I pop up the macky flapper with the large fox poly balls designed for pike fishing and they work really well. Still, sometimes the crabs pull the leader down into the rocks but this rarely happens. With the chum bag down and the chum line started I loose fed small bits of bait etc over the sides of the boat and also use a Bird feeder cage with a weight attached and regularly keep topping it up with fresh macky entrails/heads etc to keep the chum line going. Once when setting the cage feeder down a tope ripped it off the end of the rope. So I always carry a spare bird cage feeder. On a nice sunny day, tope are truly a wondrous sight as they come into view in the crystal clear blue water. Like grey ghosts, from beneath the surface of the sea. It's almost surreal to be connected to a deep-sea monster by just a thin fishing line to my absolute delight and very much the Topes annoyance. However when the Tope comes on board, probably the 1st time it has ever been stopped in its tracks they can go quite mental, pure muscle from head to tail. The sheer power has to be experienced to be believed. There is no comparison to normal big fish like pike or salmon etc. Of course, I'm much better equipped to handle/weigh them now. I use a large tarpaulin gardening bag which I find perfect for weighing and it also stops the Tope thrashing about and possibly damaging itself or anyone else for that matter. I also tag them as part of a Marine sport fish tagging programme set up by IFI in 1970. IFI supply the tagging tool and tags and all information, size, sex, location etc are logged to record the movement and distribution of a lot of the shark species. In my opinion, it's the single best commendable thing IFI has ever done and of great interest to anyone involved in catching these magnificent creatures. Recaptures of tagged Tope return around 10% which is a good enough return when you think about the dangers of the commercial fishing fleets. I even caught an already tagged Tope in 2016 and sent off the details. This particular Tope had been tagged three years previously at Bray on the east coast of Ireland. Approximately 100 kilometres from Clogherhead. The furthest recorded recaptures reported to IFI are from the Canary Islands and also Algeria both around a distance of 3000 kilometres and the longest reported recapture was twenty-five years. Amazing information and again I have to congratulate IFI and hope they can always keep this programme operating.

BASS

Bass anglers on the east coast of Ireland are a rare enough Breed of angler, probably because the bass themselves are not very plentiful at the best of times. Plus I haven't heard or know of anyone that fishes them over the winter period. I guess the bad weather we get during that period would make fishing pretty much unbearable with the cold easterly winds that sometimes last for weeks on end. Once the weather settles I'll start to target the bass from the shore. Usually from April onwards right through until November weather permitting. No need for a boat for bass fishing as I regularly catch them in only one or two foot depth of water and maybe 10 foot depth at the deeper areas. My biggest bass to date was 9lb 4oz and as luck would have it, it was the 1st bass I've ever caught. Lucky, Well I'll just add that I had spent maybe ten days per season for the previous three seasons without ever connecting with a bass so I could scarcely believe it when my spoon bait stopped in the middle of a breaking wave and started pulling my rod around in an arc until line started coiling off the drag. What's happening I thought? Well after all my efforts, finally I landed my 1st bass and what a specimen for a 1st one. So, all fired up with enthusiasm I went to the same spot the next day and caught a second one 4lb 8oz. Finally I cracked the code. I'm sure that plenty of anglers will understand as I've had enough personal text messages over the years from anglers wondering what to do, or where to go would be a more important query. Unfortunately I couldn't possibly share this hard earned information. Besides, it's many times more rewarding finding your own way through trial and error. Good numbers and sizes can be found from time to time and it's like striking gold when it happens. I'm not alone in not wanting to share any information freely. That's why I had 3 previous seasons blanking every session. I've dabbled a bit with using bait/rag/lugworm, etc and it can be very effective. But it's not for me. I regularly meet the bait lads on my travels and they do very well some days, usually catching the bigger fish, sitting behind a couple of 12ft beach casters. When you do catch it's basically just hauling the fish towards the shore and not much fight as such as the bass is dragging your 4oz gripper weight and your 12ft beach caster and possibly a raft of sea weed that's been collecting on the line while waiting for a bite. Maybe I'm missing the finer points of it but I'll stick with the lure fishing thanks. It's the tug that's the drug, an instant adrenaline shot to the brain. Boom as they say. Bass anglers are the most secretive of all of the species of the Angler, even more so than pike anglers would you believe. During your quest for your first bass this secretiveness will feed into your psyche and you'll probably find yourself part of a small group of individuals that you will only ever meet while bass fishing. They'll all tend to be loners and information will be very cautiously shared after being investigated and vetted.

I have been chasing Bass for about ten years (not counting the first three years of blanks). My best bass session to date was 2020. I caught ten in a short three hour session. All between 2lb and 3lb weight so a good size in general. I only ever keep one or two and the rest are released. My thinking on lures for bass is that it doesn't really matter for close range fishing as long as the lure is between 75mm and 125mm. Shallow diving stick baits or Rapalas for the very shallow water and jig heads with sand eel shads up to 20 grams for the deeper water and rougher conditions. White and yellow work well for me in all conditions perhaps using the smaller lighter lures in flat clear conditions and the bigger heavier jig heads in coloured choppy conditions.

East coast silver surfer. 7lbs.

Another very effective and very much overlooked lure is the flying C in any colour. It's also great for sea trout so an all round winner. It really is that simple, trust me on this as I've been through an awful lot of different lures over the years. A basic set up for bassing would be a 9ft spinning rod with a casting weight up to 30 grams, add a 4000 size spinning reel loaded with 10lb b/s mono and away you go. Keeping it simple until you start catching. Of course I still get plenty of blank days and I think that they're not around in numbers on these days. One thing I will say about these short sessions is keep casting, casting, casting as there are days when I'll just get one hit and it makes all the difference. So don't miss your chance, keep casting. It can be a bit of a slog to get the first few landed but when you do you can start to build on successful sessions and piece the jigsaw together as how and when are the best times to fish your chosen area. The single most important factor to think about is location. Where I fish, it's possible to catch anywhere along the Louth/Meath shoreline as it's all very similar. Shallow beaches and rocky outcrops, especially where beaches meet the rocky out crops, is always a good starting point. However, along the miles and miles of shoreline there are definitely some hotspots. Finding them is the key, also some spots produce over the top of the tide and some spots produce over the bottom of the tide. So, two hours before high tide until two hours after and the same with low tides. I don't fish in between bits as three or four hours casting lures is enough for me. Everyone has their own preference about tides and it's about having confidence in when and where you are fishing, which lure and the right time of the tide. Another point of interest is that twice a month there are bigger tides. I find the bigger the tides the better the fishing. There are various tide tables available online so I always plan in advance and consider the weather variation as well. Bass are definitely creatures of habit and return to the same areas on the same tides repeatedly. So, when you get all the pieces in place Bingo. But of course there's nothing set in stone so keep casting for that one bite to turn a session into a good one. Bass are another fine fish for the table too with a delicious flavour and texture unlike the farmed or frozen ones from the supermarket. It's worth the bit of effort to prepare them properly but is definitely worth scaling and boning the fillets. Once prepared I like to leave them in the fridge for at least one day or even up to five days and the flavour definitely intensifies. Try it out and you'll understand. With a little sea salt and placed onto a hot pan with a little rapeseed oil, place the bass flesh side down first. I know that it's generally recommended to put the skin side first onto the pan but what happens is that some of the skin cooks quicker and maybe burns a little and leaves some black speckle on the pan. So that when you flip it over to the flesh side the flesh side picks up the bits of burnt black off the pan and spoils the look of the white flesh. There's nothing wrong with it but I think it's a better presentation starting with the flesh side down. A couple of minutes either side of the fillet on the pan and then into the hot oven for ten minutes. Let it stand for a few minutes before eating.

MULLET

The hardest of all the fish to catch and in Ireland unfortunately the numbers are way down on what they once were. I've heard of commercial fishing boats fishing for them recently and exporting them abroad. It makes me sick that they are allowed to fish so close inshore with no regard for anything, only money. We used to catch them to decent size in 1970's Ireland. As young teenagers myself and my friends spent a lot of the summer around the local harbour at Clogherhead village. Mostly fishing for mackerel and generally messing about. When the tide was fully out in the harbour there were good numbers of large mullet casually cruising around and feeding on the discarded remains of filleted fish dumped by the trawlers. The whole harbour area was completely covered with these rotting remains. Being bored with the mackerel fishing we decided to try to catch the mullet but had been told time and again by everyone else that fished there that they couldn't be caught. Using the same tackle we used for catching mackerel on bait (mackerel strip) it took us a while to figure it out and it turned into a bit of a competition between my friends and I. I honestly can't remember who it was that cracked the method but when we did we had some great sport catching mullet up to 6 or 7lbs in weight. Of all the hundreds of rotting fillet carcasses lying on the seabed in the harbour the mullet shoal would single out one particular piece and they would all go to work on it in mid water, sucking it in and out, spending all their time on the one piece and completely ignoring any of our offerings. We did try bread and that too was ignored. We hooked some of the dead fish from the bottom and tried them as bait but they too were ignored by the mullet.

Probably by accident, I think it was myself that picked a discarded mackerel strip off the ground that had been walked into the concrete in the hot sun so it was very raggedy looking and going off in the warm sunshine. Anything was worth a try. It needed a natural presentation, or as natural as was possible and with no weight and the heavy monofilament line used for mackerel fishing it was impossible to cast without weight added. I climbed onto one of the moored trawlers and dropped the raggy mackerel strip over the side, watching it slowly sinking and waiting. Of course it would take a while but back then at that time I had all the time in the world. The strange thing about fishing for mullet is that the mullet will come and go, swimming right past your offering completely ignoring it until eventually one of them has a little taste. This is when the excitement starts to build. The water needed to be crystal clear so the bait was clearly visible. We didn't have polaroid glasses then. Watching the slowly sinking bait and trying to keep it suspended as naturally looking as possible with very gentle rod movements. (Any sudden movement on the bait and the mullet would spook and you're back to square one). Once one mullet has had a little taste then the others will soon join in and you'll have a few of them circling your bait like a little shark school about to devour but, they don't. They suck it in and blow it out in the blink of an eye (honestly it's that quick) and they keep repeating this sucking and blowing, never actually holding the bait. Eventually I realised that the only chance of hooking one was to anticipate the sucking in and set the hook if your timing was correct. Its possibly one of the very best sight fishing experiences with anticipation and excitement all in one. Waiting to see the suck and strike before the bait is discarded. We became very adept at this method and had many great sessions catching the aforementioned uncatchable. Like I said, the blink of an eye is all the time you get to set the hook. Sometimes catching maybe a dozen big mullet over the low water period between us.

It's important to remember that the mullet will completely ignore anything you are offering for maybe up to an hour (which is why most people give up) But you must stick with the plan if they are there in front of you, eventually you'll get a response. And once one of them has a taste the others should follow and keep coming back for more. I don't know why this is the case but there are some things in fishing and in life that we'll never know about, and that's the thing about fishing that keeps us interested.

Sun holidays are always great for a spot of mullet fishing as the mullet thrive in the warmer waters of the Mediterranean Sea / Canary Islands, etc and anywhere south of Ireland.

Of course the first things packed for a sun holiday is my fishing tackle, travel telescopic rods etc and enough bits and pieces to cover any fishing opportunities that may arise.

I was to learn a very effective way of catching mullet while on honeymoon in Turkey in 1998. The purist anglers among us will not like the following method much but the fishermen/women most definitely will. If you are of a sensitive angling disposition maybe skip the next few pages.

I always love the little fishing trips while on sun holidays abroad as you never know what you're going to catch and even more amazing is being able to communicate with other nationalities (kindred souls) through fishing hand signals and grunts etc. Sometimes even speaking English, but usually not. Getting up at first light, while Caroline and the kids are still tucked up in bed I could grab a couple of hours fishing. It's worth considering where your accommodation is situated when booking any sun holidays and for me the closer to the seafront the better.

On my honeymoon in Turkey I somehow teamed up with a local man that couldn't speak any English at all and we went mullet fishing off a rocky headland fishing into the wide open sea. Nothing like the harbour fishing usually associated with mullet.

Ali's tackle consisted of a beer bottle with about 100 meters of line wrapped around it but it was the rig at the business end that was the important part. We stopped at a local bakery and bought 6 loaves of bread which he had examined thoroughly before buying.

I'll try to explain the rig as best I can. A small barrel swivel at one end of a 15 inch leader with approximately ten hooks (size 10-12 long shanks are best), tied in every Inch and a half or so. Attach the swivel to the mainline. Break off a fist sized piece of fresh bread. French baguettes are ideal because of their doughy inside and they hold together better in the water. Tear the crust on one side and open it, roll it tightly around the swivel so that the crust is on the inside of the roll and the white fluffy bread is on the outside, trying to keep the bread as fluffy as possible. Then wrapping your leader tightly around the bread so that the hooks are standing off the bread and using the last hook to stitch into it and knitting it all together. Gently cast the bread and leave it to drift as naturally as possible with no sudden movements (as I mentioned before mullet are easily spooked). It may take a while to get any interest and the mullet can completely ignore your bait and any free loosely fed pieces of bread. I've seen this happen even with great numbers of mullet swimming around. Then for no apparent reason one mullet will start to taste the bread and soon enough the others will join in. Sometimes turning into a feeding frenzy pulling at the bait from all angles. The trick with this method is not to strike because with multiple mullets pulling at the bread from all angles eventually one will pull a hook into another one and then tighten up slowly. Not strictly angling I know but still some sport to be had. Ali did manage to catch one around 3lb and lost a similar one. None for me but a new method learned and I'm always a willing scholar. When we got back to Ali's shop he was parading up and down with the mullet held high over his head to great applause from locals and tourists alike, bizarre.

We cooked a couple of them in the oven on one of our holidays to the canary islands and have to say that it was some of the best table fish I've ever had, probably due to the clean Atlantic waters around the islands .

The effectiveness of Ali's rig is such that on one sun holiday Caroline and Abygail were sunbathing on the beach so myself and Tommy went for a walk around to the local harbour to see if there was anything about. Sure enough there were good numbers of decent sized mullet so out came the telescopics and the bread rolls that pretty much come everywhere with me when I'm on holidays. There were a good few people fishing and enjoying the hot sunshine. It took about five minutes and we landed a nice mullet. I probably only had one cast for that fish. Another cast or two and another mullet landed much to the interest of the other anglers who were mostly holidaying like myself. One of the younger ones from the group came over for a chat and wondered how we caught the mullet, so I explained the rig and he was very interested as they had been trying every method to catch one of these mullet for the whole of their two week holiday, with no success. He said Tommy and I had made them all look a bit rubbish. Apparently there was no tackle shop in the resort and he offered me a tenner for the rig which I politely refused. So, the moral of the story I guess is to always make sure you're well geared up for the old sun holidays.

TRAWLER STORY

Back in 1980's Ireland, things were so much different. Money was scarce, as were jobs, as they were once called. Most of my generation were forced to emigrate to England and America which offered better opportunities at that time. A twenty year old me lost my petrol station job due to change of ownership. I remember being unemployed and having only the shoes I was wearing. No second pair for occasional wear. One pair of shoes (Trainers). There was me and two older brothers, my sister plus my Mother (Eileen) and Father and grandmother living in our 2 up 2 down townhouse. My Dad Tom worked steadily to keep us going. It was all very normal at the time being perpetually skint. (no money) Back then if you did happen to get a job you would quit school at an early age, so no college degrees etc. All normal for us and our peers and I don't think that we knew a single person that went onto third level education.

I was offered a start on a local trawler fishing out of Clogherhead Harbour just seven miles from where we lived in Drogheda. We had all heard about the big bucks to be made by the local fishermen fishing prawns so off I went on my first trawler trip. Interviews had not been invented for this type of employment. I met one of the deck hands and he told me (every second word spoken by these trawler men is usually an expletive of some sort so I won't bother to add them here) *"Meet us in the Sail Inn at 6 o'clock on Sunday evening and don't be late."* The Sail Inn was about two miles from the harbour.

Arriving at the pub at 6 o'clock I met the rest of the crew, me being the 5th member. The skipper asked me what I was having. *"Pint of Carlsberg, thanks."* Followed by another, and another and so on. Trawler men have a great reputation as savage drinkers as with all sea going men. It felt like an entry level exam to see if I could hold my porter.

At about 1 o'clock in the morning we all spilled out of the pub into a car and away down to the harbour and onto the trawler. She was called *The Village Maid* and she was a right old rust bucket. For the rest of the crew this was all part of their daily grind, But for me, I could hardly believe I was setting sail in the middle of the night, on a rust bucket of a trawler with a steaming drunk crew. Skipper said to get some sleep now as we'll be steaming out to the fishing grounds for four hours. I did try to sleep but it was never going to happen the first time out. The bunks were like something you would see on a famine ship. My bunk right next to the engine room and extremely noisy plus, the bottom half of the mattress was damp from where I could see water leaking through the side of the hull. At least it was during the summer and not too cold. Then, all up on deck, shooting the nets, finally starting to fish. We were fishing for prawns. This involves dragging heavily weighted nets across the sea bed for four or five hours, scooping up prawns and whatever else happens to get in the way. When the net is hauled in and emptied its shot out again to maximise fishing time while the crew sort the catch, tailing prawns (removing the heads from the tails, these days the heads are left on) They were very affordable then and it would be unusual to eat less than a dozen or more at a sitting. Today you'll be lucky to pay a lot of money for two or three as a starter course.

The hauling, emptying, shooting and tailing carries on like this around the clock, twenty-four hours with an hour break every haul for something to eat or a nap maybe. Not a job for the softer variety of mankind.

By around 6pm on Monday evening the sea was starting to get a bit lumpier. With no sleep or comfort I was wondering when we were going back to the harbour. We hauled the net and shot it again and the sea was getting rougher. So, I asked when were we going back? The skipper replied, *"when we fill the hold"* (where all the catch is stored on ice underneath the deck space) *"Oh!"* I said in disbelief, *"How long will that take?"* *"As long as it takes,"* he said, *"Maybe a few days."*

No mobile phones or internet back then so no contact with family etc. What did amaze me as we trawled somewhere in the middle of the Irish sea, all around our boat I could see the lights from other boats fishing the same areas. There must have been thirty or so lights visible at any one time. Sadly the Irish Sea has been overfished for decades and now bigger boats are needed to travel greater distances and the price of prawns almost makes them too expensive to make a decent meal.

Meal times on board were very basic with a pot of spuds and butter and guess what, the fish of the day. No fancy cooking required, everything boiled in seawater. Prawns and cod. We would take the biggest jumbo prawns from the last haul and I have to say they were a real treat, straight from the seabed and onto the plate with a little salt and you definitely will not taste better than that.

So, on it went, hauling, shooting, emptying, tailing prawns.

Two of the other crew members were suffering sea sickness from the lumpy sea and spent most of their time vomiting, luckily it didn't affect me.

There were reasons unknown to me previously as to how I ended up as a crew member on this supposedly jinxed trawler. None of the local fishermen would go out on it. That explained the novice seamen vomiting their guts up. Basically we had a ramshackle crew of men trying to earn a few extra shekels. The previous skipper had had a heart attack on board and died and also in the previous month while shooting the nets some of the hauling gear parted from the deck and badly injured a crew member's leg. They said he was lucky not to lose the leg completely. It was damaged so severely.

As a result. the local fishermen were giving this boat a wide berth. No pun intended. We had two Drawda (Drogheda) men, One Fecker (from Termonfeckin) and two clawher lads (Clogherhead).

Just as it was getting light on the Wednesday morning and during one of our short breaks we were all summoned up on deck. The nets were snagged on the bottom and we were using the hauling gear to try and free us. The net was pulling the back of the boat down into the waves. I swear to God I thought it was the end of me.

Recently, in the news there had been two trawlers, one of which from Clogherhead, had disappeared in the same area (Irish Sea) and were suspected to be sunk as a result of getting their nets snagged in a supposedly Russian submarine. As it turned out one sinking was admitted by the royal navy. In 1982 during the Falklands war the HMS Porpoise was monitoring the Irish Sea for Soviet sub activity and snagged the nets of the Clogherhead trawler, The Sheralga, skippered by Clawher man, Raymond McEvoy. The British Government refused to pay compensation but eventually compensation was granted. Luckily all five crew members survived, rescued by nearby trawlers.

I was full sure we were stuck in a sub and after what seemed like an eternity of pulling with the hauling gear, eventually it broke free of the bottom and all that came back was half of the net.

I was left manning the helm for the return journey while the rest of the crew got their heads down. I only had very basic navigation equipment, and I thoroughly enjoyed it. A few hours later we docked at Clogherhead harbour and unloaded our catch onto a waiting lorry. It was around 11.30am and the weather was fair. The skipper said that he would be getting new nets sorted and would meet back here around 7.30pm. I had different ideas but agreed with him anyway. I staggered away from the harbour as my inner ear was adjusting to being back on land. That was the end of my trawler fishing career and it turns out that I too am one of the softer varieties of mankind.

Finally, I hope that the stories and shared knowledge will help in some way on your own angling adventures.

Tight lines, David.

Guiding services are available for any of the species covered in this book. Contact David Dennis on social media, email: daviddennis@live.ie or Mobile: 0866082822

Fisherman's prayer.

God grant that I may fish, until my dying day,
And when it comes to my last cast, I humbly pray,
That in the Lords safe landing net, I'm peacefully asleep,
And in his mercy, I will be judged, big enough to keep.

(author unknown)